Gracie and the Mountain

Growing Young Climbing Mount Le Conte

Emilie Ervin Powell

**Revised and expanded edition based on
Grace McNicol's diaries, with many photographs**

The Overmountain Press

The lodge on Mount Le Conte, franchised to Stokely Hospitality Enterprises by the National Park Service, still operates as of 1996. Managed by Tim Line, the lodge takes reservations for the next year beginning October 1. Usually booked by mid-October, openings do occur throughout the year due to cancellations. Le Conte Lodge may be contacted in writing at 250 Apple Valley Road, Sevierville, TN 37862, or by telephoning 423-429-5704.

ISBN 1-57072-053-3
Original Copyright 1981 by Emilie Ervin Powell
Revision Copyright 1996 by Emilie Ervin Powell
All Rights Reserved
Printed in the United States of America

2 3 4 5 6 7 8 9 0

*Dedicated to Sam and Julia
in memory of our days along the trail.*

Foreword

My interest in writing this book began when I met Grace McNicol by chance at the National Park Service Sugarlands Visitor Center near Gatlinburg. As enthusiasts of Mount Le Conte in the Great Smoky Mountains, my husband, Sam, and I decided to attend a slide show on the mountain at the visitor center.

The presenter showed many slides, including one of an 87-year-old woman, Grace McNicol, who had climbed the mountain 201 times, more than anyone except employees at the lodge on top. Explaining that she was present, he asked her to stand. She popped up in the back of the room with a big smile.

After the show, we talked to Grace McNicol in the lobby and told her that we had climbed the mountain eight times, starting when we were students at the University of Tennessee at nearby Knoxville. I was immediately struck by her animated conversation, especially about the mountain. She was slender, alert, and moved with alacrity. She appeared more like someone in her sixties than eighties.

We talked with her about Herrick Brown, who had been operating the lodge the last time we had climbed the mountain. She explained that he had retired and was living on Mount Rogers in North Carolina. That night I telephoned Herrick, asking him about the frequent guest.

"She's just truly remarkable," Herrick said. "One of the things I miss about Le Conte is getting to visit with her about once a month…. She loves nature and communicates her enthusiasm instantly. She was a hit with almost everyone, no matter where they came from."

As editor of a magazine for a textile company at the time, I thought my readers might enjoy learning about Grace McNicol. I traveled to Maryville, Tennessee, to interview her about the many climbs of Mount Le Conte. The session lasted almost eight hours and was recorded on tape. She told me that she was going up the mountain again in about three weeks and suggested that I come along. She was going to ride up on a horse and hike down an eight-mile trail.

I wanted to see her in action but had been having trouble with my back and ankle and feared I wasn't up to it. I told Gracie that I didn't think I could ride the horse and explained that I'd had trouble with horses as a child.

"Don't you do a lot of things better now than you did as a child?" she asked. It was true that my fear of riding a bicycle had been overcome, but extreme depression set in with the realization that at the age of 45 I would have trouble matching the physical accomplishments of an 87-year-old woman. The challenge was accepted and reservations were made for me at the lodge in early November of 1977. Gracie showed me more on Mount Le Conte than I had ever imagined possible on my previous eight visits there.

I was soon writing the story of Gracie and her mountain in the Great Smokies. We talked by telephone and visited together several times.

I published a small biography in 1981, which has sold primarily at Sugarlands Visitor Center in the Great Smoky Mountains National Park. I have received letters and calls from readers all over the United States and two foreign countries. People asked about Gracie and confided that reading the book encouraged them to try hiking for the first time. Many said they were trying to get in shape to climb Mount Le Conte. "I found the grass of parnassus below the spring on Le Conte just where Gracie said it was in the book," one woman told me.

Following Gracie's death in 1991, her family gave me access to diaries that she began keeping during the years she worked in Alaska. I found they provide even more insight into her unusual life than the facts she revealed to me. A highly-religious woman, her diaries show that her faith sustained her in difficulties through the years. She overcame many hardships to achieve her successes, both in nursing and climbing the mountain.

This revised and expanded edition, based on Grace McNicol's innermost thoughts as recorded in her diaries, gives a much more vivid insight into her remarkable life than the original work.

Blazings . . .

Pulling up Stakes at Sixty-Two

"It's cabin fever," the Seattle physician told the 62-year-old nurse from Sitka, Alaska, who complained of exhaustion and comprehension problems in January of 1954.

Grace McNicol knew she would have to change her lifestyle, because during the past eight years she had cared for many longtime sufferers of cabin fever at Sitka's Pioneer Home Hospital, so-named since the patients were aged and sick men who had come to Alaska as pioneers in the gold rush days. But she, like most persons, had not recognized the symptoms in herself. After all, the old prospectors had deserted families in the United States years before and lived alone in the bush, pursuing what usually proved fruitless dreams of riches.

The Kansas-born nurse had found life challenging and exciting when she arrived in 1945. She had relished long walks alone along the roads of the 100-by-75-mile Baranof Island, she said, "until I learned the grizzly bear stories were true."

She had enjoyed many weekends as a guest in the homes of friends and vacationed stateside once each year, but the snow, rainfall, and general lack of sunshine had finally taken their toll. During the long rainy seasons, the nurses at Pioneer Home had eventually learned to wear their raincoats and galoshes all the time.

"On the few sunny days teachers would dismiss school so the children could play outside, rejoicing in the golden rays,"

Gracie recalled.

Despite the long nights of Alaskan twilight and isolation, the nurse had delighted in sparkling green spruce trees and islands floating in the blue water turned red in rare sunsets.

But in early January of 1954, the physician said she must not return to her job in Alaska. "Travel," the daughter of Scotch immigrants replied when he asked what she liked best in life.

"Then travel," he advised.

She spent another week at the home of her sister Estella in Seattle. Estella had stored a lot of Gracie's belongings during her years in Alaska. She had lived frugally in one room in the nurses' quarters at Pioneer Home. Pictures, mementos, even extra clothing were stored at Estella's.

Gracie spent a whole day sorting and packing in the basement room designated as her storage space. She carefully sorted through pen and ink drawings by an Eskimo artist that she had followed throughout her years in Alaska. She added some ivory pieces and brass plates to the trunk.

The January 13 entry in her diary summed up her feelings: "I'm hoping someday to have a place to call 'home' and have all my things in that place. But will I ever? Yes. I'll find my way as I travel. I know I will. I'll go first to Aunt Nora's in Portland, Oregon and buy the bus ticket for my trip there."

Gracie left Seattle on January 29 in fog and rain very typical of Sitka. Carrying the usual Alaska wet weather togs, she took the seat behind the driver and looked forward to a short visit with Aunt Nora and weeks of traveling as she decided where to begin a new existence. She gave no thought to retiring, although most persons at the age of 62 had a date in mind.

Having been sickly through her teenage years and having spent most of her thirties convalescing from intestinal problems, Gracie had been a strong, healthy, practicing nurse since age 40. "After such a late start, I was of no mind to quit and I thought registered nurses were in demand most places," she recalled.

Three crisp, white nurse's uniforms were packed in her

suitcase. As the Greyhound bus rolled on toward Portland, she recalled the past year with much ambivalence. She had been sick for most of April 1953 and did not improve even after spending a week in the home of a friend, getting completely away from the Pioneers Home. The hospital physician had recommended that she take her annual month-long vacation in the States, going first to Seattle to visit her sister and to see her longtime physician there.

"A month won't do it," her Seattle doctor had said. He had insisted that she not return to her job in Alaska for three months. Gracie had called the Pioneers Home physician and made the arrangements for two months extended leave without pay following the month of paid vacation. She would resume her duties at the hospital in August. Living in a single room at the nurse's home in Alaska and taking many meals there for the past eight years, she had accumulated savings that would finance such a sabbatical.

As the rain beat upon the bus window, Gracie reached into her purse for her diary, a hardback book with room for entries for five years under each date. When she lived stateside, she never thought of keeping a diary. But the isolation in Alaska made the diary welcome at the end of each day or shift at the hospital. She had missed few entries since 1947.

She looked at her entries for 1953, seeing that she had left Seattle immediately after seeing the doctor that time also and traveled quickly by bus to Lost Springs, Kansas, which had been her family's home since her parents homesteaded there in the late 1800s. Her brother Wesley and his wife, Lorena, still operated the nursery started by her mother and father.

Wesley met her at the bus station, and Gracie walked out into the fields as soon as she reached the nursery. On May 9 she wrote: "The April rain had called up the wildflowers on the fields, some of them still covered with the original prairie grass. I could barely see the fences. It was like being on the prairie again...with red, blue, white and yellow wildflowers peeping up through the green grass. I lay on my back in the grass and swooned in the sweet fragrance of the wildflowers. The sky was a true Kansas blue...a blue you never see anywhere else. I was home again."

As May breezes warmed the countryside, Gacie and Wesley planted petunias and marigolds on the graves of their parents, recalling their love for all growing things.

The daily entries recorded visits with sisters, brothers, aunts, uncles, more than a dozen nieces and nephews, and several cousins. The time eased by in a whirlwind of ball games, watermelon cuttings, and picnic suppers. She had traveled with various relatives to Manhattan, Wichita, and Herington.

But by early July 1953 Gracie began to feel stifled by the flat land which ran straight into the horizon all the way around. As she pushed wheat with her bare feet inside the wagon bed to help Wesley and Lorena harvest the grain on a hot day, she longed for the cool breezes of Sitka. She wanted to lift her eyes up and see the green spruce trees on the slopes of Mount Vestoria that towered over Baranoff Island.

"I'm going to be back at work by August 1," she wrote. And she made it, traveling by bus back to Estella's in Seattle and then flying to Juneau and transferring to a coastal plane for the flight to Sitka, arriving by early evening July 30.

"Talked with Knight at the Old Pioneers Home and he advised me to give it another try. If it doesn't work out, he said to give them enough notice to find another nurse. Tomorrow I'll be in the ward again. Courage. God be with me...guide and keep me," was the entry for July 31.

Entries in her diary always noted the shift she had worked that day: "8-4," "2-10," "4-12," and "12-8." Nurses rotated, working each shift at least two weeks at a time, sometimes more, depending on when employees were on leave or sick. She started off working the 8-4, but was soon into the 12 midnight to 8:00 a.m. shift, which proved hardest for her. She was a light sleeper and was typically awakened several times during the day as she tried to sleep from 9:00 a.m. to 4:00 p.m.

"B.D. was having a new lock put on her door and they were hammering at one o'clock. I tried reading myself back to sleep but couldn't...Jesus, give me strength," she wrote.

That night she explained how tired she was to Carl Krook, a steady male nurse with whom she enjoyed working. "He suggests that we go walking almost every afternoon at 4:00 p.m. when I try to wake up and get dressed each day. He knows I'm afraid to walk by myself because of the bears. He says I can take a nap from about 9:00 to 11:00 p.m. to get ready for work. That's what he does."

For the next few weeks almost every entry recorded an outing with an exclamation point. "Walked to Sitka Park! Took a long walk on the forest islands and climbed the tower... sunshine bright and breeze warm! Hiked down Halibut Road and picked some raspberries! Went to the old house foundation that overlooks the bay...the waves were whitecapping!

"We both had a day off and walked up Indian River past the power house...then returned to the nurses home and played Chinese checkers. He thinks he can beat me but so far my reputation as champ is intact."

Two weeks later, Gracie joyfully recorded, "We were both off on the same day again, and decided to climb Mount Vestoria. I had never even thought of doing that.

"It took us four and one-half hours to walk to the top. We could see in all directions. It was clear and sunshiny...we almost felt like we could lift our arms and fly out over the bay. I had a real urge to soar. Carl said that he felt that way too. We walked down in three and one-half hours. A wonderful day...thank God for my many blessings, especially Carl."

Three days later she wrote: "Hard time sleeping. The children outside were hollering to each other about lost balls all afternoon. Carl came by at 4:00 p.m. and we walked three miles on the trail beside Indian River. As we sat resting on a rock he told me that he has a new job in Sweden and will be leaving in about a month! Who will I walk with when he is gone? I have never known anyone like Carl. Although I was tired, I could not manage to sleep a wink before going on duty at midnight. Courage."

The diary shows that they climbed Mount Vestoria again,

this time going through a heavy rain shower. On another afternoon, they climbed to Blue Lake to see the rapids. One entry said that Carl had finally beaten her in a Chinese checker game.

An entry in late September recalled: "We said goodbye to Carl as he boarded the coastal plane to start his long journey to Sweden. He'll visit friends and relatives in the States on the first leg of it. Louise took me to her house for a chicken dinner...such kindness. But the blues were taking over by the time I returned to the nurses home. Courage."

Trying to keep up her daily walks, Gracie hiked a short distance to the house of her friend Louise. The diary recorded. "I saw a huge flock of geese rising up over the bay. We sat drinking tea and watching a beautiful red sunset."

Job stress crept back into the daily entries. "Hard work on the floor. Forty-one patients and each one needs something different. At mealtimes it's so hard to keep up with who wants sugar, who doesn't, who needs to have their meat cut, and so on.

"Remember, Christ is the light of the world. Let him shine through you to others. Look up."

As the bus zoomed along, Gracie wrote Carl Krook's name on her notepad several times. She returned to the diary, shaking her head at the troubled entries of the previous year.

"Can see snow on the mountain tops now...up where Carl and I looked out over the world. What will this winter bring? Another nightmare on the floor today. When Sara and Nick are supposed to be helping me, I have more work to do. They should rotate off Friday."

"A real equinox storm. No plane for a week...so eager to get a letter from Lorena. So tired and sleepy while on 12-8 duty. Everything out of place. I tried to straighten up, but didn't finish. Courage."

"I don't seem to have patience with those I work with anymore. Sometimes it seems like we let these old men at Pioneer run the hospital. I told B. D. we nurses should say how we feel things should be. But she's not one to rock the boat. Slept only four hours today...ate a good supper but can't seem to go to sleep now. Lord, guide me. Help me to keep my mouth shut."

The depression was strong in the next diary entries:

"Boris was supposed to help me on the night shift, but he didn't come until 2:00 a.m. I felt more dead than alive tonight. We have babied these old men patients until there is no end to what they ask. Letter from Carl the only bright note. He's reached Stockholm. If only we could hit the trails in snow shoes. Remember, prayer is the answer."

"Work. Try to sleep in spite of all the noise around here. Work again. Nurses have the hardest work. Why did I ever become a nurse? I don't know. Lord, help me to see thy purpose. Courage."

Gracie reread these entries. What had happened to her in 1953? Optimism had been the hallmark of her life. She had often been assigned to troubled wards because of her ability to cheer people. Her performance had not been criticized during the time of those entries. Was B. D. just being sensitive to the fact that she was depressed? Although she had not been fond of her supervisor, Gracie credited her with being a fine nurse.

Gracie wrote an entry in her diary: "Greyhound is only 50 miles from Portland. The fog is breaking up. Nursing is my life. I know I can do good work again...if I can find a warm place with lots of people around. If I can find a place where it's safe for me to walk by myself...where I won't have to rely on other people who have their own lives to live. God be my guide."

Gracie recalled taking the Baranoff boat to Seattle, filled with sorrow as she bid goodbyes to her longtime friends in Sitka. As she left Alaska, she had feared she would be unable to return, and that's how it had worked out. Now she sought a new life somewhere in the rest of the U.S.A.

The sun was shining when Gracie stepped off the bus in Portland. She postponed telephoning Aunt Nora to come for her, and instead went straight to the ticket counter. She bought a round-trip bus ticket from Portland via San Diego, California; Key West, Florida; Knoxville, Tennessee; and Portland, Maine. The cost was $218.20. She had worked very hard to accumulate savings. Now she would enjoy them and at the same time find a new job and new life. She would begin her long trip in one week. The round-trip ticket was tucked securely in her billfold.

Grace Viola McNicol began her long trip with a very scenic ride from Eugene, Oregon, to Mount Shasta, which was covered in heavy snow. She continued on through the central part of California. Gracie had already visited most of the major cities and recreational areas of the United States and Canadian provinces during vacations of the past 20 years. She always traveled by bus and stopped at various places for stays with her six brothers and sisters.

Never owning a car or even learning to drive ("Why waste the time and money...I can go anywhere I wish," she'd tell friends), she would ask bus drivers and terminal personnel to steer her to places of interest, thereby finding regional highlights not featured in tourist guidebooks, which she also consulted.

Most vacations had been solo by choice. "That way I could do as I pleased," she said. An incident in Las Vegas on this trip leaving Alaska illustrates some of the benefits of traveling alone with little luggage. Having been advised nothing was available in Las Vegas on Saturday night, Gracie began talking with a clerk in a large hotel. He suggested that she could stay free in the room of a couple checking out at midnight until the arrival of persons with reservations for it the next day. His offer was good only if she agreed to "keep quiet" about the favor.

"I didn't bother anything...just slept in my clothes on top of the spread until he called early in the morning. I don't have trouble sleeping as a rule, except when working night shift. I probably tipped him a dollar as I usually do people who are extra nice."

While at Aunt Nora's, Gracie had decided to stop over in Long Beach, California, where she had worked in a hospital for more than 10 years before going to Alaska. She telephoned ahead, making arrangements to spend a couple of nights with Bertha Trembly, the sister-in-law of her ex-husband.

Her marriage was one subject Gracie almost never discussed with even the closest friends and family. She and Fred Bennett Trembly, a musician, were married in Long Beach on May 13, 1935. He obtained a divorce in Las Vegas, Nevada, on March 2, 1943, on charges of cruelty. Gracie did not contest the divorce.

She reached Long Beach on February 17 and spent the night at the Alexandria Hotel, paying $2.50 for the room. In the evening she had dinner with an old friend who was still working as a nurse at the Long Beach hospital. They recalled the old days and "caught up" on the whereabouts of most of their fellow workers.

Gracie took a city bus to Bertha's on January 17. She and Bertha spent the 18th visiting old friends. Gracie recorded on the 20th in her diary: "I was washing clothes in the kitchen and talking to Bertha when Fred Trembly walked in. We were both surprised. He gave me a big hug and we visited awhile and ate lunch together. Then he left and Bertha and I went shopping. He returned and had dinner with us.

"He talks to me while watching television with Bertha and a friend who dropped by. Then we all visited and listened to Fred and Charles play the violin and guitar. It was like old times. I love to hear their music.

"I was rather upset and didn't put too much trust in our talk because I don't want to hurt Fred nor wish for him to hurt me. We weren't alone together so we didn't bring up the past and argue about things. It's upsetting to see him again. He wanted to see me alone but I told him I think we should continue to go our separate ways as we have done these past years. I told him that I would write to him when I get to Lillian's and I will.

"I couldn't make him happier than he is. He goes about and plays music at beer parlors and takes his friends in his car. I live a completely different life. I wouldn't be happy living his way. So we parted as friends and I decided to go on before I cause any trouble. Fred offered to take me to the bus.

I refused and Bertha's husband took me."

But later, when Gracie was in Knoxville, Tennessee, on May 13, she wrote in her diary, as she did every year on that date: "Remembering that wonderful day in 1935."

Back in 1949 in Alaska, after recording the usual remembrance on May 13, Gracie wrote: "But in spirit I am now free. If you feel bound by another person, you need to gain your freedom first of all in your own mind and heart. Leave everything in God's hands. He will watch over us."

From Long Beach Gracie rode the bus to Leucadia, where she was met at the station by relatives Dan and Lillian McNicol. Seventeen letters had been forwarded there by Estella in Seattle. Gracie had made elaborate plans to visit relatives and close friends all along the way. Estella would forward any mail for Gracie that came to her, since Gracie had listed her as a forwarding address from Alaska.

Gracie, Lillian, and Dan enjoyed a day at the zoo in Balboa Park in San Diego. "I stayed an extra day with them and we strolled on a wet beach, basking in the sunshine and watching the breakers and birds. Alaska seems so far away," she wrote. The diary records nothing about Gracie writing Fred as she had promised.

Before leaving Leucadia, Gracie briefly considered going to Hawaii, the only U.S. state that she had not visited. "But the nurses' registrar advised me against it, saying too many nurses were going over to avoid cold winters in the United States. Nursing jobs were not opening up for newcomers."

Leaving California, her next stop was El Paso. "Three miles walking in Carlsbad Caverns…so beautiful and interesting. And the tour of Juarez, Mexico was worthwhile. Most different were the adobe buildings everywhere…hard to understand how they can make them with mud, straw and water."

Her diary recorded many more interesting adobe buildings on her next two stops: Sante Fe and Taos, New Mexico. She stayed at the Del Vargis Hotel in Sante Fe for $2.50 and extensively toured museums and shops selling Indian art. "I bargained for a silver necklace and the Navajo came down from $1.95 to $1.00."

In Taos, she toured the ancient pueblo and attended a lecture on its history and an exhibit of oil paintings on the pueblo and the city. Throughout her travels, Gracie tried to learn as much as she could about any area that she was in. She visited most museums and took commercial tours when they were offered. She took every free brochure and asked numerous questions.

From Taos, she took Greyhound to Canon City, Colorado, to spend a few days with her brother Ralph. Gracie felt tired and slept all night and until noon the next day. She and Ralph played Chinese checkers after enjoying Lula's dinner.

Growing reflective at bedtime, she made a long entry in her diary: "Do be careful and obey God always. I feel that I haven't lived as close to God as I should. I know I haven't in my travels as I go and see places and am so busy entertaining myself that I leave God out of my plans. He is so good to watch over me at all times and how ungrateful I am of His goodness to me."

Gracie bade Ralph goodbye and boarded the bus in Pueblo, Colorado, at 7:14 a.m. "Now I'm headed for the wide open spaces," she wrote in her diary.

She arrived in Wichita, Kansas, at 9:40 p.m., and immediately checked into the McClellan Hotel, where the room rate was $3.50. She was up early the next morning and spent the day with her sister Minnie in a suburb.

On March 17, Gracie went to the nurses' registry and found an old friend, Elsie Kimble Porter, in charge. "Although it cost $50.00 for the city registry and $18.00 for the national, I decided to pay it. I think I'll try it for a short while until I earn $50 to count in this quarter for my social security. I got work for this very night—a private duty stroke case at Wesley Hospital," was the entry.

Next day, she wrote, "After a long day I managed to sleep only one hour before going on duty at 10:45 p.m. last night. I had to learn where everything was as you always do, and I even got nervous taking the patient's blood pressure. But I got along all right. All credit to God. My prayers were answered."

Gracie rented a room across the street from the hospital for $1.75 per night. "There isn't too much noise during the day so I am sleeping fairly well. Called Minnie. Hope to see her again on my night off. I have another private duty case at St. Francis Hospital, a 63-year-old man recovering from a heart attack. He had a convulsion last night. Work very hard. The floor nurse helped me. I don't know what I would do if it were not for the kindness of others." She continued working for two more weeks.

"My patient died at 3:52 a.m. Very sad. Had so much to do that I didn't get away until late. I think I've made enough money to move on and visit the folks awhile. God, help and guide me."

On April 8 she arrived by bus in McPherson, Kansas, to visit with her brother Fred and his family. Ralph and Lula came in from Canon City the same day.

Gracie rode with Ralph and Lula to Wesley's home in Lost Springs on April 10. "We all went out to see Wesley's lambs. He has over 30, weighing from 90 to 112 pounds. The wheat is up more than usual for this time of year. Wesley doesn't have as much as he used to because of the government regulations...soil bank I think."

The entry for April 14: "Ate black walnuts; saw young chicks, talked to a red bird, and packed Mother's silver to mail to Ruth. So many memories being in the old home place again."

Returning to Wichita on March 17, Gracie resumed her long vacation by bus. As they rolled along, she wrote: "Getting near Joplin, Missouri. The wheat is higher than any place along the trip. The red bud trees are fully in bloom and many trees have leaves. Will spend three days in Springfield with Juanita."

"We went to the Assembly of God Church and heard a story about a couple that had drifted away from the church, but then returned. They were welcomed and helped to change their lives. A big lesson to learn...to always lend a helping hand to those in trouble," was the next entry.

Her trip continued on through Little Rock, Arkansas; Lake

Charles, Louisiana; and on to New Orleans, arriving April 23. She got a room at the LaSalle Hotel for $3.00 a night. She paid $7.50 for four LaSalle tours and was soon seeing the entire city. Her entries recorded architecture in the French quarter, flowers blooming throughout, cemeteries with tombs above ground, and the site of the Battle of New Orleans.

"I took one night tour. I enjoyed the musicians on the street, but did not enjoy the one night club that we visited. I paid $1.30 for one glass of 7-Up. They had a show during dinner. I couldn't stand any more such shows. Too wicked for me. I regret that I saw one. I felt unclean. I read about Jesus raising Lazarus before going to sleep. How wonderful is our Christ and we fail to follow his teachings."

Another tour was from the LaSalle Hotel by Greyhound. It covered some 200 miles traveling in the area between New Orleans and the Gulf. Gracie filled eight pages in her diary documenting all that she saw. One entry listed flowers: "Oleander, wisteria, roses, azaleas, spirea, gardenias, hibiscus, hydrangea, passion flowers, and magnolias...with Spanish moss in all the trees. I saw a 500-year-old live oak with limbs 125 feet long."

The next stops were Mobile, Alabama, and Pensacola and Tallahassee, Florida. After two nights in Tampa, she arrived in St. Petersburg on April 30. There she rode a city bus and then walked six blocks to visit the Tabernacle of Moses in the Wilderness. "I rested in the garden and listened to the chimes of hymns. I went inside the church at three o'clock. A motto on the wall said, 'He that is mastered by Christ is master of every circumstance,'" she wrote that evening. "Saw a most beautiful sunset. The sun was a yellowish, orange ball sinking into the water. White, fluffy clouds drifted in the east."

Gracie stopped off at Cypress Gardens in Winter Haven on the way to Miami. She decided against spending $38.00 to tour Havana, Cuba, instead departing for Key West. "Wonderful to see the banyan trees with the limbs growing into roots. Drove on many bridges to Key West with the ocean on both sides. Seeing so much water makes me long for Sitka."

Next came the Everglades, where Gracie spent five pages

recording the plants, animals, and birds that she saw. "Flamingos, macaws, parrots...at one place I had my picture taken holding a big monkey.... It's like a jungle."

Spending the night again in Miami, she noted that it was time to be getting on to Knoxville, Tennessee. Her youngest sister, Ruth, lived in the country around Oak Ridge. Her husband, George, had gone there in 1943 to work in atomic installations, and it became their permanent home.

She rode the Greyhound on U.S. Highway No. 1, with many breathtaking views of the ocean as they passed through Daytona Beach and Saint Augustine, where she enjoyed turtle soup while watching porpoises leap into the air. She spent the next night at the Aragon Hotel in Jacksonville for $2.30.

"Between Jacksonville and Augusta, Georgia saw almost nothing all along the roads but unpainted shacks, with Negroes working in the fields. Everyone wearing raggedy clothes. You'd think a house would be painted once in a while, but I don't remember seeing one. Such poverty is almost unbelievable in the United States. God love them."

The next night was in Greenville, South Carolina. "Five dollars for a room at the Greenville Hotel was outrageous, but at 9:15 p.m. I had no choice. I was really very tired."

"Good to see the mountains again," she wrote as the bus neared Asheville, North Carolina. Soon she was in the Great Smoky Mountains. "Dogwood is blooming all over the mountain sides. The leaves are not out as much here. The mountains continue on and on, one ridge after another. It is sort of hazy—maybe that's smoky."

Gracie arrived in Knoxville on May 7. Being unable reach Ruth by phone, she decided to take the bus to Oak Ridge. "A real estate man that I met in the station gave me a ride out to Ruth's...said he was going that way. When we drove up, Ruth was chasing a calf in the pasture. I got out and helped her catch it. The salesman laughed and laughed. Guess he was surprised to see a 62-year-old woman overtake a calf. Later Ruth teased me for picking up a man."

Sleeping until noon the next day, Gracie arose to find four

suitcases and a lot of mail forwarded by Estella. "Ann writes from the Old Pioneers Home, asking me to come back. Makes me a little homesick. But I know I can't return. The doctor was right. Traveling really did help me. I'm sleeping better than I have in more than a year. And I can keep my mind on things. I was having a hard time concentrating in Alaska.

"Now I've got to unpack all these suitcases and try to find something to do with everything. Someday I hope to have a home some place for all my things. But first I must find a job. I know not what the future will bring, but I know that my heart will sing because I am in God's hands. I shall go forward, upright, and free, because He will walk the way with me. He is mindful of his own."

Swapping tales of mountain climbing would become a favorite pastime for Gracie when she began climbing Mount Le Conte in Great Smoky Mountains National Park.

On the job at Blount Memorial Hospital, Gracie gets ready to check on her patients.

Finding a New Job and a Mountain

Gracie's handwriting was bold on May 12 when she recorded this entry: "Went to the nurses' registrar in Knoxville. I asked about general nursing in small hospitals in small towns. She didn't know of anything. Then I went to Children's Hospital in Knoxville and filled out an application. A nurse there told me that she had heard they were looking for a nurse in Sevierville, a small town at the foot of the Great Smoky Mountains. Courage. Keep looking up."

Gracie had always enjoyed visiting her youngest sister while delighting in the lush greenery of undulating Tennessee hills that rippled gently across the landscape in the Knoxville area, becoming gradually higher until they rolled upward into the Great Smoky Mountains National Park some 50 miles to the southeast. The 500,000-acre parkland is an emerald of forested wilderness crowning the Tennessee-North Carolina border, with its highest peaks above 6,500 feet.

Ruth drove Gracie to Sevierville on a bright, sunny day. As they neared Sevierville the outline of the Smokies rose in the distance. "I'd love to see that on the way to work every day," declared Gracie. But the hospital had just hired a new nurse and anticipated no more openings. However, they had heard of the need for a nurse at Blount Memorial Hospital in Maryville, another small town in the foothills of the Smokies about 30 miles away.

They traveled to Maryville the next day, soon finding Blount Memorial Hospital atop a hill on the eastern side of town. As they walked to the door from the parking lot, Gracie saw the Great Smoky Mountains rising up on the horizion. "What a wonderful spot," she exclaimed. Blount Memorial was looking for a nurse. Gracie filled out a long application. She talked with the head nurse for almost two hours. The head nurse delved deeply into Gracie's experience, from her first job in Kansas to her years at Long Beach and then in Alaska. She asked many questions about her experience in obstetrics at Magnolia Hospital in Long Beach in 1945. They said they would take her application into consideration.

Back at Ruth's, Gracie continued to sort through her things. She had at least four more suitcases at Estella's but had written her to wait until she got settled into a new job to send them along. And then there was the unused portion of the bus ticket that would take her through Portland, Maine, and then back across the country to Portland, Oregon.

Gracie and Ruth began trying to let out the seams in Gracie's nursing uniforms. "I've gained 15 pounds since I left Seattle. I guess it was the relaxation and all the good meals that I have eaten. I'm up to 160 on my 5-foot-eight-inch frame. Too much! I've never been this heavy. I've got to cut back...but how can I and eat at Ruth's table? Everything's so good. But when I get a room, it won't be hard."

Blount Memorial called, asking her to come the next day to talk again with the head nurse. Gracie took a suitcase, thinking she'd probably go to work.

But the nurse just asked her a lot more questions about her experience and asked her how she would handle certain types of situations. They said they would be in touch later.

Feeling confident of getting a job sooner or later, Gracie and Ruth looked for a room. They found one at 212 High Street. The room had been rented by a Blount Memorial employee who had moved out the day before. It had kitchen privileges and cross ventilation. It was also within walking distance of the hospital and downtown Maryville, where the bus station was located. Gracie wanted to be near a bus station, which would serve as a base for her travels.

On June 1, Head Nurse Moles phoned and asked Gracie to come in that day if possible for a physical examination that would include lab work at the hospital and a checkup by a physician. Gracie and Ruth drove to Maryville, taking three suitcases, including the enlarged uniforms.

The diary entry for June 2 read: "I went to the hospital and they said the physical showed I was in good health, especially for a 62-year-old woman. I start working tomorrow on the 2-10 in the maternity ward. I guess that is why she asked so many questions about my experience in obstetrics in Long Beach. The pay is low, only $2.15 per hour with 10 and 20 cents extra for evening and night shifts. But living costs are lower here than in Alaska. I should make it even though I am paying for my room. I can fix food in the kitchen here and save money. I owe so much to Ruth and everyone for their kindness in helping me to find the job and get settled in this room. I'm thankful to my Jesus for His help and guidance."

After her first day at work, the entry read: "It's hard to start working again, but all are so nice to me. As usual, it's hard to find where they keep everything. But I got a good start today. I think I'm going to like this type of work. The mothers and babies are well and happy. I sure don't miss those fussy old men at the Pioneers Home. Thanks be to God for all my blessings."

Before going to work on June 5, Gracie walked downtown and bought blue jeans, a man's shirt, a cap, and a small shoulder pack. While having lunch in her room at noon, she wrote in her diary: "My hiking clothes are still at Estella's. With the duds I got today I am all set to go hiking in the Smokies. I phoned the park service and they say a hike will be going up the Alum Cave Bluffs trail on June 8, my day off. The ranger will lead a group, starting from the trail head just off U. S. Highway 441."

On Tuesday, June 8, the veteran bus traveler arose early and rode 15 miles from Maryville to Knoxville to catch the bus going over the mountains to North Carolina. The total mileage would be about 65 one way.

She was enjoying the mountain scenery when she realized that the bus had passed the Alum Cave Bluffs Trail parking lot. The driver said they were about a mile above the trail head. Undaunted, Gracie got off the bus and walked back to the trail head, only to find that the ranger and his group had already departed.

Gracie set out on the trail to catch up. The sign said the distance to Alum Cave was two and one-half miles. She was accustomed to being alone and was at least acquainted with the Great Smokies, having traveled through the park several times over the years on her way to visit Ruth. And she knew there were only black bears in the Smokies, which did not pose a threat like the grizzly bears in Alaska.

Striding along at a brisk pace beneath rhododendron bushes that arched together five and six feet above her head, Gracie listened with enchantment to the waters of Alum Cave Creek rippling over boulders and splashing invitingly as she crossed log footbridges. She lay on the spongy bank and drank from a crystal pool reflecting a lacy green hemlock which reached up from the forest floor at least 50 feet.

Later she would recall a feeling of belonging, even on that first day as she climbed the trail. She didn't know then that she was on the side of a mountain that would become a challenge and joy for the remainder of her long life, but she was immediately captivated.

"I guess it was the trees, and plants and flowers...so many...so green and beautiful everywhere you looked from the tiny partridge berry to the giant trees. I grew up learning to love trees in my father's nursery, and I loved growing things the way he did," she recalled.

Yellow birch waved to her as she climbed higher, their light trunks silhouetted against darker foliage and boulders. She realized that it was going to rain and remembered that she hadn't brought a raincoat or sweater. But she didn't worry and soon was filled with delight to reach a large heath bald glowing with delicate rose-pink rhododendron blooms. The rain was now heavy, but the sight of the flowers warmed Gracie enough to keep her going upward to join her party.

"All I could see was the top of your head, soaking wet, coming up the steps," the park ranger would say for years, recalling that day Gracie finally reached the group of about 15 hikers waiting under Alum Cave Bluffs for the rain to stop.

At 62 she was the oldest person in the group, and one man insisted that they build a fire under the shelter of the cave, actually an overhanging mountain bluff of black slate, and wait until she "dried out."

"I wouldn't hear of it, because I knew I'd be all right...probably better off than the women who were wearing dresses. My jeans and long-sleeved shirt provided some insulation. Besides, I didn't want to stay in that dirty place," she recalled. Since the bluff overhang is 20 to 25 feet, the rain seldom or never dampens the ground, which is usually powdery and yellowish, the result of the decomposition of the slate that contains iron sulfide.

As they waited, the ranger explained that they were about three miles from the summit of Mount Le Conte, which at 6,593 feet above sea level is one of the highest and steepest slopes in the eastern United States. He said that on the following week he would lead a group to the lodge on top and stay overnight. "I'm going to be off again. Count me in," Gracie told him.

The sun came out as the party walked back down the trail from Alum Cave. Gracie had about 30 minutes to rest before catching the Trailways bus on Highway 441 that took her through Gatlinburg and on to Knoxville. She barely made the bus to Maryville, arriving there about 7:00 p.m.

The diary shows that she continued to work the 2-10 shift and that she was becoming fond of her co-workers. "This is really a nice group. Kindness for someone new on the staff really makes you feel at home. Remember to return that kindness at all times."

Gracie washed and ironed her new hiking clothes and packed food to take on her trip to Mount Le Conte. She must supply her lunch each day, but dinner and breakfast would be provided by the lodge. June 14 found her up at 6:30 a.m. to begin the bus trip to Knoxville to catch the over-the-mountain bus. She met the ranger and a party of 23 at the Alum Cave Bluffs Trail head at 9:30 a.m.

Some clumps of white rhododendron were filled with blooms contrasting with the purple blooms this time. The ranger pointed out thickets of shrubbery that he called "dog hobble." He said it was so dense that dogs had trouble trying to get through it. Rain fell on the group for the last mile or so as they reached the top. Gracie was thrilled upon seeing the lodge. Le Conte has three peaks, and the lodge was in the forest between the peaks. It consisted of about 10 board-and-batten-covered cabins and two log lodges surrounding a grey-shingled dining hall. They were soon in the dining hall, meeting Pauline Huff, who operated the facility with her husband, Jack.

The lodge register shows the straightforward signature of Grace McNicol on June 14, 1954. She listed her address as Sitka, Alaska, suggesting that she probably had not quite decided to stay at Blount Memorial Hospital at the time of her first hike up Le Conte.

"Pauline was a lovely person and took me over at once,"

Grace McNicol in front of the dining hall and office at Mount Le Conte Lodge.

Gracie recalled of that first stay. "She showed me to one of the cabins and built a fire so that I could dry my clothes. Before nightfall she asked me to move into the lodge and stay in the room with two women so that she could put a couple in the cabin.

"I was glad to oblige and spent the night sleeping in the bottom bunk of a large, handmade double bunk bed. It was made of balsam wood. The women took the top bunk. I really liked the Hudson Bay blankets. Their bright green, yellow, and red colors shone against the mellowed balsam walls, and I needed the warmth of a wool cover before morning. It reminded me of Alaska."

The ranger, who had explained natural features all along the trip coming up, had acquainted them with the history of the lodge. He said that Paul Adams was the first to operate the facility for the Great Smoky Mountains Conservation Association, ardent leaders in the movement to establish the national park. Adams set up operations in 1925 in a tent near a spring just below the present lodge which stands in a forest clearing on a tableland between the peaks of Cliff Top and Main Top.

Douglas Lake, Sevierville, and Knoxville are visible from the lodge on clear days. The ranger explained that the Huff family, who were operating the facility on Gracie's first stay in 1954, had taken over from Adams in 1926. Jack Huff had developed the lodge during those 28 years, erecting the single room cabins, lodges, and three-roomed dining hall. They were mostly constructed from the balsam fir trees which cover the mountaintop. The lodge is said to be the highest resort east of the Mississippi.

Gracie learned that no roads lead to the top of Le Conte— only five trails. All food and supplies were brought up by packhorse from Gatlinburg in 1954. All guests (the lodge accomodated some 50 per night) had to come either by foot or horseback. Some years later, pressures from environmental groups would force the lodge to be supplied mainly once a year by helicopter, with lamas replacing horses to bring up fresh produce. The padded feet of the lamas would not cut into the trails like the hooves of horses, which some said caused destructive erosion.

The cabins reminded Gracie of Alaskan outposts, their chinked walls grey against the background of dark, green balsam fir trees. The air was pungent with the fragrance of

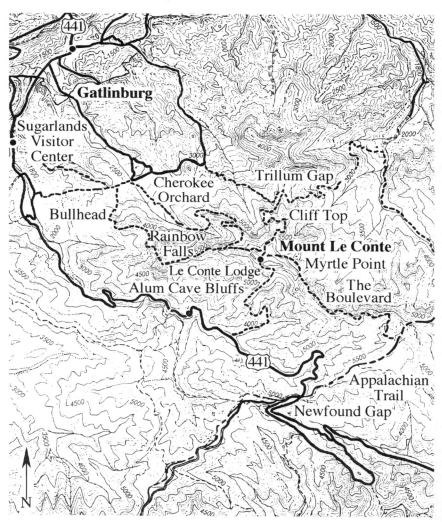

Mount Le Conte can be reached only by foot on five trails. They are Alum Cave Bluffs Trail, 5.2 miles; Boulevard Trail, 8 miles; Bullhead Trail, 7 miles; Rainbow Falls, 6.75 miles, and Trillium Gap Trail, 5 miles. Grace McNicol hiked all of these trails, many times alone, over a period of 30 years.

Mount Le Conte Lodge is in the balsam fir forest between the three peaks of the mountain. In the mid-1960s the balsam woolly adelgid appeared in the Great Smokies, and the aphids began feeding on the balsams. By 1996 many of these trees were reduced to stark skeletons.

fir, mixed occasionally with the smoke of wood fires that guests were lighting in the cabins. (A fire usually feels good at night in June on the mountaintop, where nighttime low temperatures have never been known to be higher than 60 degrees.)

The ranger explained that the Cherokee Indians, the first known inhabitants of the Great Smokies, had called the mountain Walasiyi, the place of the large, green, mythical frog, apparently never seen by white men. The green balsam trees pointed their arms horizontally and tops straight toward heaven, while under their skirts grew a solid cover of green ferns and mosses. The latter seemed to exult in the floor of decayed trees, felled by ancient storms. A green frog would find the lacy fern haven a paradise, Gracie guessed.

After a supper of canned ham, sweet potatoes, green beans, biscuits, and peaches, Gracie joined a group following a guide to see a beautiful sunset at Cliff Top on the western side. Returning to the lodge, it was too dark to see well. They lost the trail briefly and stepped in several mud holes, but they were soon in the lodges around the fires telling tall tales.

Gracie's diary tells about the next morning: "I was too excited to sleep well. Mrs. Bruhns had invited me to go to Myrtle Point to see the sunrise. But when the alarm went off and it was so dark, she backed out. I went on with eight men—was the only woman. But they didn't seem to mind. Everyone was taking pictures as the sun came up. Myrtle Point is all rock with some heath plants growing in grooves.

"We could see the mountains surrounding us in all directions...a sea of wavy green with a sort of smoky haze over everything. A junko, hermit thrush and other birds were singing. I felt like soaring out over the mountains. It has been almost a year since I looked out over the world from the top of Mount Vestoria with Carl. If only he could have been with me on Le Conte. He would have loved it. I must write him about this."

The years blur the exact moments that one later realizes must have been the beginning of a trend that determined events of life thereafter. But Gracie's first breakfast at the lodge could easily have included the moments that cast the die for her personal conquest and love affair with the mountain that lasted for the rest of her life.

When recalling her many visits to the lodge, Gracie always fairly glowed when talking about the breakfasts. Lodge guests tend to arrive exhausted at nightfall and eat dinner beside strangers while recounting the physical feats of their hikes or horseback rides up the mountain trails. Introductions are made, and some linger to share more stories of the day or past climbs and perhaps continue swapping tales in one of the lodges, or, in later times, around the stove in the recreation hall. But when morning comes to the 50-acre tableland surrounding the three peaks of the mountain and guests assemble in the shingle-covered dining hall, the hikers have become a family, albeit they hail from several different states and even foreign countries. And so it was on Gracie's first morning. Pauline Huff and her helpers were serving pancakes, all the trimmings, and coffee that temporarily eclipsed the fragrance of fir.

At breakfast the person sitting beside you in the balsam-

Breakfast is a favorite time at Le Conte Lodge. People recall yesterday's feats on the trail coming up and anticipate today's thrills on the way down. Gracie is at the head of the table, a place that came to be reserved for her through the years.

paneled dining room with its bright-checked tablecloth is the old friend from the night before and you have a common goal for the day: descending the mountain. Gracie, who at age 62 had already traveled widely by bus on her vacations, found it easy to strike up a conversation with most anyone. There probably was a feeling of family and home for each guest for 30 to 40 minutes, and perhaps it went a little deeper with her than the others on that June 15 in 1954. Despite many hardships, she was to return 243 times during the next 37 years. This was for many years the most any person other than lodge operators and employees was known to have climbed the mountain.

Gracie's diary records the end of the trip this way: "We hiked down the Boulevard Trail about eight miles to Newfound Gap. It amounted to walking mostly on top of the mountain ridge. There was a heavy cover of moss and ferns under the balsam. Before we reached Newfound Gap the trail intersected with the Appalachian Trail. It proved a hard hike because it rained most of the way.

"My shoes became soaked and the leather rubbed against my corns. I had forgotten to bring moleskin and band aids didn't stay on. I had a raincoat, but the condensation underneath made me wringing wet. The ranger had a vehicle parked at the gap as did most of the other people. I had planned to catch the bus there, but the ranger took me in his car down to the bus station in Gatlinburg. As bad as I looked, I had to get on the bus with folks who had not been walking in the rain all day. I sat on newspaper to try to keep from getting the seat wet.

"When I finally got to my room, I took a hot bath, rubbed lotion on my aching feet, and slept very soundly. I didn't get up until almost noon the next day. I had recuperated before I checked into Blount Memorial for the 2-10 shift. God is so good to create all the wonderful outdoors for us. Praise unto Him."

Gracie and friend Mrs. V.S. Wince of Newark, Ohio, start up Alum Cave Bluffs Trail in October 1964.

Learning to Talk with Chickadees and Other Joys of Solitary Hiking

Dressed in starched white cotton, Gracie strode the halls of Blount Memorial during the next two weeks, pausing occasionally on a clear day to look toward the Great Smokies outlined against the horizon. In her mind's eye she could see past the first ridges—on to the famed three peaks of Le Conte. Since the 6,593-foot mountain is connected to the main range of the Smokies by only one ridge, she could visualize the giant of the chain standing out in the smoky haze.

The nurse learned more and more about the mountain and the park during that first month in obstetrics, reading National Park Service brochures and maps and talking with hospital employees and patients, some descendants of early settlers of the Great Smokies.

Although two mountains in the park are higher—Clingman's Dome at 6,642 feet and Mount Guyot at 6,621—they are peaks on a series of mountains seemingly pushed together by some giant geologic upheaval millions of years ago. But Le Conte thrusts forward from its ancient companions, rising a mile from its base at Gatlinburg. Le Conte stands as high above its feet as the first ranges of the Rockies that Gracie had admired on her western trips. But instead of the reds, greys, and blacks of the rock mountains of the west, the top of Le Conte was lavishly clad in green balsam fir, usually wearing a filmy scarf of mist.

The register in the lodge bears the bold signature of Grace

McNicol on June 29, 1954—just two weeks after her first ascent. But this time she listed her address as Maryville, Tennessee. The abode of the mythical green frog had apparently captured her heart and was on its way to becoming her "days off."

Gracie's life pretty quickly settled on her work and what was becoming "her mountain." She was getting the hang of Blount Memorial, judging by her diary: "Even though we have 24 patients, there are enough on the staff to avoid rushing all day long. I worked in the nursery today and gave a blood transfusion to a wee thing."

Another entry: "The work is becoming somewhat easier for me as I learn more about the hospital. But I dread the responsibility of being in charge. Remember to be thoughtful, kind, enduring, forgiving and forgetting. Have tolerance for everyone. Live close to God."

On another day, the entry read: "I'm weary. I took temps at 4:00 and 8:00 p.m., passed out all the trays and collected them, and did most of the bed pans. Not a minute to spare. But I felt better today because I slept better. It was 83 degrees inside this room day before yesterday, so I went downtown and bought a fan for $17. It was a lot of money to spend, but well worth the difference it makes in here."

As the weeks went by, Gracie's diary entries continued to comment on work at Blount Memorial.

"I'm really glad the patients change often and don't stay forever like the old men at Pioneer. Mostly I just work, sleep, and eat and do it over again. I do enjoy seeing the sunsets through the hospital windows. Lately they are almost always a red or yellow ball of fire.

"Moats and Debaty are very good workers, and yet they thought I was mad at them. I was just so tired I was quiet. I must try to relax more before I break down again. I think I'm running around too much on my days off and getting tired out. Then can't sleep well in this heat. God be with me."

On her next two consecutive days off, Gracie took the bus to Ruth's and they relaxed around her sister's cool spring. But two weeks later she again climbed Le Conte on her days off, spending the night at the lodge.

She lived frugally in her room near the hospital, a practice which had become her way of life during 22 years of nursing. Unencumbered by furniture, she lived simply in furnished rooms. This enabled her to spend her days off as she pleased, having little in the room requiring attention, such as animals. But she usually had a plant or two in the window. "They could get by without a drink while I was away," Gracie explained.

She continued to hike with the park ranger's group at first, watching the ranger closely "to learn how he hiked."

"I could see there was a knack to it. You don't have to have much energy...just relax your whole self and walk in rhythm. When I realized I was tense, I would count 'one-two, one-two' until I got the rhythm."

The ranger would point out wildflowers and give their names, doing the same for other plant life and rocks. Occasionally wildlife, including the black bears of the Smokies, would cross the Alum Cave Bluffs Trail, and he would explain their habits and the probable reasons they were found in the area.

Gracie, with her childhood memories of packing tree saplings for shipment to nursery customers, liked to identify plants and animals. She enjoyed hiking with the "walking encyclopedia" in the form of the ranger. But eventually Gracie began craving a bit of solitude in hiking. "When around people I talk too much and miss too much of nature."

So she began hiking up the mountain with the park ranger's party, staying overnight, and descending alone down the seven-mile Bullhead Trail on the northwestern side of the mountain. She would telephone Bob Ogle, a Gatlinburg taxi driver, and have him meet her at the bottom of the trail in Cherokee Orchard. Bob Ogle was still driving a taxi in the resort town in 1978.

"I'd get up early and eat with the lodge crew in the kitchen before seven o'clock (in those days the crew ate breakfast together and before the tourists...in later years they would eat whenever they preferred) and be on the Bullhead no later

A few weeks after she began climbing Mount Le Conte in 1954, Gracie began hiking the five trails alone quite often. She felt she could get closer to nature, not being distracted by companions. Here she heads down Bullhead to see spring wildflowers.

than seven-thirty.

"That first summer I saw more flowers on Bullhead than we'd been finding on Alum Cave Bluffs Trail. After hiking the other three trails—Boulevard, Rainbow, and Trillium Gap—in later years, I concluded that Bullhead has the most flowers blooming at any season. And the trees are so varied and so beautiful in autumn. The trail also has more open spaces with wide vistas over the surrounding mountains."

Bullhead begins on Le Conte in balsam fir forest, drops to northern hardwoods between 5,500 and 4,500 feet, through cove hardwoods, a heath bald with pines, and into oak forests toward the end near Cherokee Orchard. That first summer Gracie walked alone down Bullhead with her eyes searching the trailsides for blooming cohosh, snakeroot, bee balm, monkshood, angelica, saxifrage, and grass of parnassus. She saw them all, plus many others, and even a few she didn't recognize. Once home, she would search her wildflower books to find the strange plants. When unable to identify them in her books, she would write to the botany department of the University of Tennessee in nearby Knoxville, giving full descriptions and the locations and elevations where the plants were growing. Within a short time, botany department personnel would answer, always giving a name for her mystery plant. Gracie continued the practice of writing the department for more than two decades.

Having no people to talk with on her trips down Bullhead, she found that the birds and squirrels would talk with her. "I'd stand perfectly still, and the birds would gradually come to me, sometimes trying to see their reflections in my glasses. I have a pretty good conversation that way when I meet up with chickadees."

She wrote in the notebook that she always carried on her hikes: "I am alone, but not alone because I am with God in the quietness of His wonderful great outdoors. His bird is calling...a red-breasted nuthatch in the pine tree...I see the white stripe."

During her thirties, when she was a near invalid in her Kansas home, Gracie had studied the birds a lot. "The black birds always came the twenty-fifth of April, and I began to look closely at them with field glasses and study their habits. But here in the southeast, the trees are so high by the time you get your glasses in line the birds are gone."

Gracie greatly enjoyed her first hike down the Rainbow Falls Trail. She recorded the happenings of the day in her diary: "After breakfast I went to Myrtle Point with a nurse and teacher. Upon arriving we talked awhile with the Scot we first met last night at Cliff Top. He was actually wearing a kilt, and I joked with him about being Scotch, since my father had immigrated to the United States from Scotland and then homesteaded in Kansas. The kilt was in a plaid something like the McNicol plaid and I asked him what clan he belonged to. He didn't seem to know much about the plaid, and I told him the name of the book in which I had found the McNicol plaid pictured. It was hot and I imagined that he was more comfortable in his skirt than I in my jeans. We all returned to the lodge by 11:00 a.m. and said our goodbyes. It was really too late to begin a seven-mile hike down Rainbow Falls Trail.

But I had already arranged for Bob Ogle to meet me in his taxi.

"I walked fast. There were so many rocks in the trail that they hurt my feet. Mountain laurel were blooming everywhere...the most I had seen on the mountain! I walked out on a narrow point called Rocky Spur. It was covered with laurel. The scenery from this point was grand indeed.

"Rainbow Falls go over a huge rock as big as a 2-story house. It appears to be granite. I could hear the water before I reached the falls. Although in a rush to reach Gatlinburg and the bus station, I took time out to eat a sandwich and apple. As I sat in the edge of the cool mist on that hot day, I recalled all that I had seen on the trip...from Myrtle Point and Cliff Top I had looked out over a vast stretch of mountains, valleys, rivers, lakes, dams and farming country. I felt alone with God in that wonderful place and looked around at his handiwork everywhere.

"Shortly after leaving the falls, I saw a mother bear in the woods beside the trail. She had three cubs up in a tree. I kept my eye on her and shuffled my feet in the gravel as I passed. I decided to start carrying a hiking stick for such occasions.

"I reached Cherokee Orchard just 30 minutes before my bus was scheduled to leave Gatlinburg. Bob Ogle was sitting there in his taxi. A welcome sight!"

Gracie talked her sister Ruth into hiking up Le Conte with her that first fall in 1954. "It was October 19 and I remember going out to Myrtle Point after a snowfall. It was the first snowfall that I'd seen on the mountain. No one had been out and everything was perfect...nothing sullied or broken or tracked. The mountain ash berries were bright red on trees below and stood out like little fires in the snow. I've never seen it like that again. Ruth and I both stood there a long time drinking in God's beautiful creation."

Ruth and some of Gracie's friends back at the hospital worried about her hiking alone. But the nurse was undaunted. "What is there to be afraid of...we don't have grizzly bears in those mountains," Gracie would respond.

And then she'd tell them about the things that you can see

when alone. Like a squirrel lying with its tummy on a limb and its four feet hanging down, watching her with bright eyes. "They would stare at me like they were hypnotized...and I'd stand perfectly still and stare back...not moving at all seemed the key. When you are hiking with other people, someone is always talking or moving. You can't get close to the wildlife at all." At other times, Gracie would mock the "chi'-chi'-chi'" mutterings of the squirrels as they stripped pine cones looking for edible seeds. The furry creatures would beam their bright eyes and echo: "chi'-chi'-chi'."

When her days off were booked for Mount Le Conte during the summers, Gracie would rise at 4:30 a.m. to catch a bus from Maryville to Knoxville and transfer to a second bus traveling to Sevierville and on through Gatlinburg up into the Great Smokies en route to North Carolina. She would get off at Alum Cave Bluffs Trail head about 8:15 a.m.

Did she ever consider buying a car? "What for? I could go anywhere I wished by bus and so much cheaper. Think of the investment and then the gas and insurance. And how could I look at the scenery and drive, too?"

By the summer of 1955, Gracie was varying her descent routes to include the Boulevard Trail, which runs along the crest of the high ridge connecting Mount Le Conte to the main range of the Great Smokies. The Boulevard runs southward from Le Conte's top to connect with the Appalachian Trail extending westward to Newfound Gap on U.S. Highway 441. Gracie would time her descent to reach the gap before the Knoxville-bound bus was due at 2:30 p.m.

The Boulevard proved quite different from the Alum Cave, Bullhead, and Rainbow Falls trails. It never fell below 5,700 feet above sea level. It was truly a walk through a northern forest, a fast trip to Canada featuring tangled heath balds and overlooks of precipitous drops into valleys below. Green ferns and moss covered the trunks of trees felled in blowdowns many years before.

It was called a darker trail because the sunlight did not filter through the continuous mantle of fir the ways it does through oaks and other hardwoods of the western and northern slopes.

"When I first began hiking the Boulevard, I had trouble with the temptation to become confused and walk in the wrong direction. Since the elevation changes only slightly, I feared getting mixed up and heading back to the lodge," Gracie recalled.

"I kept saying to myself: 'I must not get confused,' and I kept my hiking staff pointed toward Newfound Gap anytime I stopped to eat or watch the birds."

Gracie hiked the Boulevard and other Le Conte trails many days in the 1950s without encountering another person. Park visitors increased from some 2.5 million in 1954 to more than 9 million a year by 1977. It is estimated that the number of hikers increased 300 percent in that period—from approximately 200,000 to 800,000 a year.

Since her days off came during the week by choice, chances of meeting other hikers were more scant because more persons seemed to walk the trails on weekends. Gracie always enjoyed passing a few words with a backpacker or day hiker, but she preferred to talk with the squirrels, saving her "people encounters" for Blount Memorial Hospital.

Gracie's diary shows that she occasionally devoted her time off to other destinations. She toured extensively in Mammouth Cave in Kentucky, visited the Greenbrier in West Virginia, and once took a fast bus trip to Fontana Dam, which was on the edge of the Great Smokies Park. The Tennessee Valley Authority had built the dam during World War II, working 24 hours a day to get the dam generating power needed in the war effort.

Gracie rode on the bus from Maryville to Fontana with one other woman. "It was a 106-mile roundtrip. As we got near the dam, I counted 203 curves in one 12-mile stretch. The dam is the highest in the eastern United States. The rain in the mountains provides a lot of water to turn the turbines. There's so much to learn about the Great Smokies."

Gracie looked longingly at the Great Smokies in the distance as she walked to work at Blount Memorial each day. She spent much of her time off there.

Descending the Boulevard one autumn on a wet, chilly, and windy day, Gracie thought she heard a man moaning. Setting her staff on the "Newfound Gap side" of a small fir tree, she searched on both edges of the trail but found nothing.

The moan would diminish and then grow louder. She admitted that the sound and solitude began to close in and she could feel fear rising in her stomach, but her nurse's training and instincts would not let her desert. A hard gust of wind slapped against her body, sending her coattail flying, and the moan increased in intensity, coming from slightly below. Peering through the drizzle she saw that the trunks of two birch trees were rubbing against each other as the wind blew, producing the moaning sound.

"I think I must have laughed out loud at my own fear," she recalled. "It was so obvious once I saw the trees."

Recording the incident in her diary the next day, Gracie wrote: "Must write to Carl and tell him how afraid I was for a moment. I've been bragging to him about how safe it is in the Smokies. He's promised to come and hike with me to Le Conte when he returns to the United States. But is he ever coming back? I don't know."

Sudden storms were a reality of hiking that Gracie learned to accept as they happened. Although prepared for a rainy ascent up Le Conte by way of Alum Cave Bluffs one April, she encountered fierce winds and a downpour a quarter mile above the bluffs. It was a heavy storm.

"Water spilled over ledges and ran down the mountainside where I'd never seen it drain before. The trail itself was like a branch...had to be so careful trying to stay on the sides of the trail and step on stones that I almost missed seeing beautiful clumps of bluets and sweet white violets. I had to hold on tight when I reached the three cables [guides and handholes on a sheer rock face near the top].

"The tree tops were thrashing below the bluffs, and the wind came in thrusts like it was trying to knock me off the stone pathway cut into the rock. When I reached the horse gate at the summit, the balsams were threshing so wildly their roots caused the ground to heave. Fearing I would blow away, I lay on the ground and entwined my arms around the post, holding tight and praying.

"When the wind finally died down, I went on to the lodge. The fire never has been warmer than on that late afternoon. My clothes, pack, shoes...everything was soaked. I went to bed while another guest hung the clothes to dry. My shoes stayed wet. Some guests who had reservations that night didn't show up."

The black bears of the Smokies are the delights of park visitors, especially children, and in the 1950s people were disobeying park rules against feeding the animals. The bears naturally began to associate people with food. The majority of bears tended to frequent garbage cans on U.S. Highway 441 through the center of the park. Occasionally tourists along the highway would be severely scratched by bears while trying to feed them or take their pictures. One or two bears would usually come to eat scraps in the lodge dump atop Le Conte after dinner each evening.

Guests at the lodge usually kept their distance, perching on higher ground while the bears dined in the lodge garbage pit. Edible garbage has been packed down the mountain first by horse and then llama since the mid-1970s, but items left by tourists in trash cans in the cabins still attract bears to the dump. If bears seem to be getting restless in the pit, a worker at the lodge usually runs up with a broom, flailing away. The bears always run away from the broom.

Once, lodge guests watched a mother bear drive five cubs to the top of a giant balsam. The cubs peered down at her while she searched for food. The guests concluded that the mother bear must have adopted orphaned cubs of another female, since having five offspring would be highly unusual for a bear. Seeing the plight of the hungry mother, a kitchen worker came out with a dishpan of scraps. "Don't tell the environmentalists," he told the onlookers. "This mama bear has a lot of mouths to feed."

"Count on us," they called back, clapping.

Gracie encountered a number of bears on the Le Conte

trails at various times. "The first one I met alone was near the head of the Alum Cave Trail in the 1950s...he'd probably been visiting the garbage cans out on the highway. He was just walking in the trail ahead of me, and I decided to follow, but soon thought better of that. What if he stopped around a curve and I came up behind and scared him?

"So I grabbed a broomstick someone had discarded alongside the trail and hit it on a rock, hollering 'whhooooo, whhooooooooo.' I never speak because they are used to people's voices and think you are going to feed them. I relied on my 'whhooing' to fool him into thinking I'm something else. I guess it worked. He scampered off into a rhododendron thicket.

"I still have that broomstick today," laughed Gracie. "I can tell you, it's been many a mile because I've carried it so much. Those black bears always run away when I go into my act with the stick. I'd have been afraid to try it on a grizzly in Alaska...but these bears are much smaller."

The Great Smokies, like all national parks, is a vast garden belonging to all citizens of the United States. Through the years it has become the most visited national park, with the majority of its owners viewing the beauty from their automobile windows as they traverse Highway 441 from Cherokee, North Carolina, to Gatlinburg.

Gracie, having chosen to marvel at the wonders of her garden by direct contact with its trees, ferns, and flowers, found her own special place in the first few years of walking the Alum Cave Bluffs Trail. It's the spot above Alum Cave Bluffs when the hiker first sees the top of Le Conte's western peak, Cliff Top. It's a serene picture framed in rhododendron and lacy branches of hemlock that border the trail.

"I call that place Gracie's Pulpit, and I always stop there and thank God for creating all this beauty for us humans to enjoy. 'Peace that passeth all understanding' is possible for me when I sit there viewing the peak, which is sometimes wrapped in wisps of pink to violet mist.

"I like to recite to myself my favorite verse from the Bible: 'I will lift up mine eyes unto the hills, from whence cometh my help. My help cometh from the Lord, which made heaven and earth,'" she explained.

Just reaching Gracie's Pulpit itself was to become a major goal for the nurse later in life as she struggled to overcome hardships undreamed of in her sixties.

The lodge usually opened in April during the late 1950s, when Pauline Huff operated it with the aid of staff. Her husband had taken over the lodge from Paul Adams in 1926 and erected the buildings, using balsam logs cut from the forest atop the mountain. The double bunk beds were also fashioned from balsam, along with some tables in the cabins. Jack and Pauline, married at sunrise at Myrtle Point in 1934, ran the lodge together through 1949, when he took over operation of the Mountain View Hotel in Gatlinburg following his father's death.

Gracie greatly enjoyed talking with Pauline about her many years on the mountain. "I'd always gone with the other guests to Cliff Top on the western peak to view the sunset, but one day Pauline suggested that I might be surprised at the spectacle from Myrtle Point, a flat shelf on the eastern peak where guests traditionally view the sunrise.

"So I went up over Main Top to Myrtle Point—it's about a mile—and waited by myself. As usual, all the other guests had gone to Cliff Top. I sat on a big rock to write up my notes for the day and watch the sun go down behind the peaks far beyond Sugarland Mountain. As I began writing, the blue of the day mellowed until the bowl of the sky was aglow in yellowish pink.

"It's easy to write on buses, and I've made a habit of taking notes on my trips. I've always made notes on each hike up Le Conte, numbering the trips. On that October day I had two wonderful surprises to add to my jottings: a golden-cerise sunset whose rays touched the tops of the trees on Anakeesta Ridge with a soft glow while a yellow harvest moon rose in the east at the same time."

Gracie recalled that she sat still as the dusk moved in, filling the depths of Huggins' Hell, the dense jungle of rhododendron and laurel below the point, with dark shadows. As the moon rose higher in the east it turned from gold to silver and lighted her way back to the lodge.

Through the years she was to return alone many times to Myrtle Point at sunset time, while other lodge guests made the traditional trek to Cliff Top, west of the lodge. Sometimes Gracie joined them.

A solitary sunset vigil on Myrtle Point was interrupted one summer when she heard noises in the sand myrtle and turned to see a mother bear and two cubs.

"I hit my stick on a rock and did a lot of 'whhooooing,' but she kept coming and growled when I stood in the path. Knowing mothers with cubs are easily alarmed, I stepped aside. The bear family passed by, heading for Main Top and on to the lodge to look for dinner scraps, I guessed."

Gracie said that it was Pauline who told her she could find grass of parnassus blooming beside the Trillium Gap Trail a short distance from the spring below the lodge. The white, fluted petals of the wildflower, which is not a grass in spite of its name, sparkle like jewels among moss-covered rocks and ferns in a wet area where water begins to collect from the frequent rainfall on Le Conte. Farther down the mountain such rivulets become Roaring Fork Creek, which quite often lives up to its name while rushing through Gatlinburg. The grass of parnassus "showing" during August and September was to put Gracie on that short walk atop the mountain almost every year for more than three decades.

When Gracie's 65th birthday arrived on October 1, 1956, nothing was said about retirement at Blount Memorial Hospital. She was making rounds as a floor nurse, her five-foot-six frame trim as usual at 111 pounds and her blue eyes sparkling as she checked mothers and babies. She had lost the weight accumulated in 1954 and "taken up" all her uniforms. In those days retirement at 65 was the rule in most places, but registered nurses were in short supply.

Gracie entertained no thought of giving up nursing. "It was always my ambition, but I was a long time getting started professionally. Mother used to go help the sick people in our community in Kansas. I'd go with her, and as I grew older

Short hair seemed to be in style when Gracie was a student in a teacher's college in 1918. After graduating and teaching one year, she entered nursing school, becoming a registered nurse, her lifelong profession.

I'd go and provide help myself. Then after getting a teacher's certificate—which my father insisted upon—and teaching one year, I decided my life's work must be nursing. So I enrolled at a nursing school connected with a hospital in Wichita, and graduated in 1924 at the age of 32, being late because of sickness throughout my teenage years.

"After three years of private duty nursing, I became very ill and had to quit. At the time they thought I had some kind of intestinal problem, but later doctors theorized that it may have been complications from a ruptured appendix. I never had surgery; I was just terribly ill, completely bedridden for almost two years, and had to learn to walk again.

"They screened a porch so that I could sleep out there year-round to get the fresh air—that's the way they treated you in those days. And I did learn to love the fresh air, even in winter when the temperature fell below zero. I had my bed covered with suitable coverlets and kept warm with no problem."

After five years of recuperation—at the age of 40—she decided her health would permit full-time work again and moved to Dodge City, Kansas, to nurse in a hospital serving World War I veterans and their wives. "The hardest part was learning to give hypodermics again, but after I got the syringe in my hands it worked out all right," she recalled.

Gracie soon decided to move to Long Beach, California, because an aunt lived there and because she was able to get a general duty assignment in a hospital. The native Kansan

29-foot Richardson with one bedroom, a bath, and a modern kitchenette. She soon had the yard filled with flowering shrubs and enough plant-filled pots for every corner of the trailer in the wintertime. "I couldn't change a fuse at first, but within a few years I could do anything.

"Sometimes I had so much yard work to do that I would skip going to Mount Le Conte on my days off. But not too often, because I had to see my gardens on the mountain," she recalled.

One thing that she didn't buy was a television set. "Wherever I go I see people sitting in front of them growing old. They won't even get up to change a channel if they don't like the program. I have my radio and I can be working while I listen to it. You won't find me wasting my life in front of a television set. I don't have time for that," she explained.

Gracie and a young couple chat outside a multi-bedroom cabin at Mount Le Conte Lodge. Many of the cabins are a single room with two double-bunk beds.

The 500-Mile Year

When Gracie looked back over the years, she expressed appreciation for many friends, expecially hikers.

"You know, sometimes people will come into your life and do you a lot of good. That's what happened when I met Eula Fry of Maryville. I needed her when I met her in 1960, and I think she needed me."

Eula, a school teacher who had not worked in several years, asked to hike with Gracie following the death of her husband. The couple had hiked a lot together and then camped after his heart trouble made such exercise too hazardous. Eula's 12-year-old son didn't like to hike at all, preferring his peers as is typical of that age.

Eula was 49 and Gracie 69 years old when they met. The younger woman could take only day hikes, wishing to be home at night with son Dickey. She was unable to join Gracie on her overnight hikes to Le Conte. But the two hiked some of the trails on Le Conte by day, including a trek one February on Alum Cave Bluffs Trail.

"The snow was three feet deep around the 'pulpit' and up to the cables where you have to hang on as you round the cliffs. Well, we kept going and my galoshes had more snow inside than out, and we had to stomp the snow in order to edge along the cliffs. Realizing that the snow was slowing us down, we abandoned our plans to reach the top that day and turned back. Walking as fast as we could through the deep snow, we were unable to get out to the highway before dark.

"The car lights picked up whitecaps on Little River as we drove alongside, and we saw a fox. The weather was so bad we had the mountains to ourselves otherwise," Gracie remembered.

One day the two women had some extra time and hiked 20 miles—from Newfound Gap to Tri-Corner Knob to Smokemont. That's the longest distance Gracie had hiked in one day. "So far," she added with a big grin, as she told the story.

Sometimes they tried little-used trails like a shortcut to the Rich Mountain fire tower. Undaunted by trees which had fallen across the trail in many places—apparently debris from a storm—they crawled under or over them.

The October day was too beautiful to turn back. Gracie wrote in her notebook: "We seem to be on the wrong trail to the tower, but we see the power line...stopping past an old wooden bridge for lunch. It's clear, sunny and very warm for October...saw asters, goldenrod, closed gentians and foxglove this morning."

The next notebook entry, recorded that evening, recalled: "We found the trail on top of the ridge and walked along, with Dry Valley spread out below us on one side and Cades Cove on the other. Eula heard a rattlesnake and we listened. It sounded like big flies buzzing. We found it ahead coiled in the middle of the trail. We stood very still and it finally crawled away. The warm temperature must have delayed his search for a winter home."

Gracie and Eula hiked between Newfound and Davenport gaps, trails around Cosby, Mt. Cammerer, and Mt. Sterling, in the Cataloochee area—in fact on most of the trails in the Great Smokies park that would fit a one-day hike. They also took some trails in the nearby Tellico area. Those hikes, plus Gracie's 10 solos up Mount Le Conte in 1961, totaled more than 500 miles.

"I was never sick at all that year. When my days off came around each week, I was ready to go and Eula usually had something planned. Sometimes another friend, Millie Shields, went with us," recalled Gracie.

the formal gardens, greenhouse, and the great outdoors which surrounds the mansion. The grounds were landscaped by Frederick Law Olmstead, the famous New York architect. They were perfect and included naturalized plantings of rhododendron, laurel, and azaleas in addition to many rose gardens. The roses were in full bloom. I never saw as many different colors anywhere.

"The greenhouse was filled with orchids and tuberous begonias. Wish Ruth could see them, she loves both of those flowers. We toured three pottery and weaving shops. I really studied the weaving...strands of yarn were threaded in a maze. Most of their wool yarn comes from Australia and Scotland. They dye most of it themselves [Gracie devoted five pages to describing the weaving rooms].

"Saw many sourwood trees as we began the climb to Mount Mitchell. Also saw poplar, ash, and oak. I climbed the tower on top of the mountain but couldn't see anything because we were in the clouds. It is 6,684 feet...not too much higher than Le Conte! The Blue Ridge Mountains were really blue as we came back down from the peak of Mount Mitchell. They were covered with haze.

"We traveled 115 miles today to Chimney Rock and Lake Lure. Saw beautiful homes surrounded by gardens. A beautiful panorama unfolded at Chimney Rock, which appears to be made of granite. Lake Lure has an emerald color that reminds me of the lakes in the Canadian Rockies. I saw a rain coming up the valley and soon we were covered in a downpour. It stopped and a beautiful rainbow appeared in front and below us. It seemed close enough to reach out and touch.

"God is good and wonderful to let us see such beauty in the great outdoors. It made me think of our lives...sometimes filled with sadness and troubles and then...suddenly goodness and brightness! I was satisfied to be still for a bit and drink in that beautiful scenery. I said goodbye to my newfound friends on the tours, and left at 6:00 p.m. to cross the mountains to attend the outdoor drama 'Unto These Hills' at Cherokee, North Carolina.

"I could see Mount Pisgah standing up higher than the other mountains and I wanted to go to its top. But there was no time, if I was going to make the show in Cherokee.

"Was delighted to find the outdoor theater fitted into a natural bowl of hemlock, maple, rhododendron, laurel, azalea, and dogwoods. The acoustics were almost perfect...I don't think I missed a word of the tragic story of the Indian Tsali. A full moon shone as the play ended.

"I was very tired and slept some as the bus crossed the mountains headed for Knoxville, which we reached a little after midnight. There would be no bus to Maryville before morning. So I got a room at the Monday Hotel for $2.50. Didn't sleep too well...kept reminding myself to get up early to catch the Maryville bus so I could go home and change before going to work at 2:00 p.m."

The next day's entry was brief: "Had to drink a lot of coffee at Blount Memorial yesterday and was surely glad to see 10:00 p.m. come. I went home, took a bath, and slept like a baby. Feel much better today. Think I had better not go anywhere on my next two days off. Seems like I've been on the go forever.

"The fields and grounds at the Biltmore reminded me of our nursery back in Kansas. The McNicols were always outside, even us women. We seven children helped in the nursery, setting out plants and packing plants for shipping. I was the fourth child of the seven, the middle child that folks say gets overlooked sometimes. But I don't think I was.

"When I worked with Mother or Dad packing the plants, we would talk about all the family plans. Dad wanted each of his children to go to college and he often talked of the importance of higher education, although he never went to college.

"We would go as a family to revival camp meetings, usually taking a picnic lunch. Mother always fried about three chickens and made potato salad. We loved it...there was seldom a bite left in the picnic basket."

The James McNicol family always enjoyed being outdoors—in their nursery at Lost Springs, Kansas, or on a picnic like this at a revival camp meeting in about 1905. James and Henrietta are on the extreme right. Gracie is fifth from right.

Gracie waits for the boat in her sunsuit while on a trip down the Colorado River in the Grand Canyon in the late 1950s.

One Too Many Wild Rivers

In addition to spending her days off in the Great Smokies and taking bus trips like the one to Asheville, Gracie also pursued another hobby begun during her years in Alaska: rafting and boat trips down wild rivers in the Grand Canyon and other western locations.

"I learned about wild river trips once when talking to a bus driver near Crater of the Moon National Monument. I asked him what was the most interesting thing to do around there, and he answered: 'Shooting the rapids on the River of No Return.'

"When I told him that's what I wanted to do, he insisted it was too dangerous for anyone my age...I was about 60 then. So the next year when I saw an advertisement for a wild river trip in a western magazine, I wrote for particulars. That's how I began taking trips with Don Harrison and Jack Bernnan," said Gracie.

Gracie was one of Don and Jack's "River Rats" on seven week-long trips: five on the Colorado River (two of those in the Grand Canyon) and one each on the Green and Salmon rivers. Gracie said that Don and Jack were like most people who are in the woods or running rivers a lot by themselves— very quiet and given to speaking to the point when they do talk.

They accepted her right away, she recalled, but other passengers were not as hospitable. One man asked if her folks knew she was going down a dangerous river. On another occasion a disgruntled man blurted: "Huh, I thought I was getting away from the womenfolk!"

"I told him he'd regret what he had said because I could be the most independent person there is. Well, he didn't answer then, but before the trip was over he aplogized, saying that I'd been a good sport," Gracie recalled with a twinkle.

Jack and Don provided most of the boats, all food, and sleeping bags. Their passengers usually brought only the fee, their clothes, and nerve. Some brought their own boats or rafts.

Gracie described the thrill of rapid running as "Action. The rapids will toss you up and then down and then maybe you'll go into a wave and it'll souse you and you'll be soaking wet...only to dry out in the next stretch of smooth water or when walking around on the sand at night waiting for the guides to fix supper.

"Sometimes you have to bail the boat out, if the water accumulates too much. Each rapid is different so that you don't know exactly what to expect. The downward draw of the river is irresistible."

Eighteen years after her last trip, Gracie's blue eyes flashed as she recalled the thrill of rapid riding. "Don told me once that you never overcome being a 'river rat,' and I have found he was right. When I see the waters of the Little Tennessee and Pigeon rivers in the Smokies tumbling over boulders into those trout pools...I think of what it would be like to be shooting the rapids again."

Gracie's diary records one of the trips that she enjoyed the most. That was when she shot the rapids on the Middle Fork of the Salmon River in Idaho in August of 1951 while working in Alaska. The entries included:

"Glad that I decided to spend a couple of weeks at the Double K Mountain Ranch near Mount Ranier to rest up before taking the river trip. I was the only guest here when I arrived, but now there's a bunch: Kay, Grace, and Florie from Cleveland, Ohio; Blanche, Long Beach, California; Jay, Washington, D. C.; Denny, Seattle; and Louise, Yakima.

"We are taking long horseback rides every day. Riding

reminds me of the days on the farm at home. But the streams are so different from Kansas! Yesterday we rode beside a swift mountain stream tumbling over round rocks and stones. Then we had to cross.

"It was a queer sensation to be on a horse stumbling over the rocks in the swift water. Twice my horse Bow was belly deep but I managed to stay on okay. The wrangler didn't have to help me like she did some of the others. On the way back to the ranch Bow was scared by a hornet and started running. Soon all the horses were running. I stood up in the stirrups and stayed on all right. Some of the others were bouncing up and down so they said their bottoms were hurting afterwards.

"Got back in time for a sun bath before dinner. So far I've managed to take a sun bath every day. Sure feels good to a Sitka woman! I'm getting a tan. They are calling us women "the harem." But we don't care. It's a fine group.

"As we went higher and higher on our ride today we came into an open meadowland. We could see a wide scope of the country all around, and the glacier on Mount Ranier. The glacier was bluish and white. White clouds were hovering around it. I can't take pictures of everything that I see...so I sat still on Bow imprinting it in my mind.

"'The harem' just relaxed around the fire tonight, smelling the fragrance of the burning wood and recalling some of our exploits on the daily horseback rides. Most said they were a little afraid of the horses at first, but now everyone feels like an experienced rider. We promised to stay in touch with each other and try to meet again at another ranch somewhere. They'll take us to Yakima tomorrow and I'll catch the bus for Salt Lake City to join the Brennans for the river trip. I feel the pull of the river already."

Rested and tanned, Gracie arrived in Salt Lake City at 8:50 p.m. and spent the night in a hotel. She was up at 4:30 a.m. and was picked up by the Brennans at 6:30. It was a party of 10 heading for the Salmon River.

"We crossed the East Salmon River several times and saw Mount Borah, the highest mountain in Idaho. We spent the night before launching sleeping under a full moon on the sand beside the river. The sleeping bag felt warm around me and the sand was a comfortable 'mattress.'

"Spent the first night of the trip down river at Middlefork Rapid, and the second night at Sulphur and Dagger falls. There were high rock cliffs on both sides and big rocks in the stream. Don and Jack cooked a delicious supper and breakfast. The guides decided not to shoot Dagger Falls. We all pitched in and carried the boats and baggage up and around the falls to quiet water on the other side. They cut little trees and lashed them to the boats and baggage. It made it easier to carry them.

"Third night slept in a pup tent with May. Guess they thought it might rain but it didn't. Saw rabbits and a badger. Crawling in and out of the pup tent was a new experience. I took a spit bath in a kettle. The doctor in our party fell into the river and we all laughed. I've resolved to watch my step.

"Fourth day out. Went over several 4-foot falls today. It was breathtaking. We're camping at Sheepeater Camp. The guidebook says a hot sulphur spring is near but we couldn't find it. Jack told us the elevation was 6500 at the start of the trip and will be 3500 at the end. We are really going down! Saw many trees with red leaves already. The rocks are reddish and yellow. The rapids seem bigger now.

"Fifth Day. Met some other groups on the river today. They were fishing. Had a good time talking with them. Passed Dagger, Pistol, and Indian creek bridges. We were pelted by rain and hail as we clung to our rafts in the river. We tried to dry out by the fire tonight, but I still feel damp. Don warmed us up with the best hot tea I ever tasted. He said he brewed it with some special herbs.

"Sixth Day out. Passed through hills bare except for sage. Then saw banks covered with pine forests. Saw a kingfisher, a tanager, and large hawk circling overhead. We are spending tonight at McCall's ranch on the river bank. Everyone took a bath. We laughed about how different we look now.

"Seventh Day. Writing this by lantern light, lying on my

belly in the pup tent. We sat around the camp fire under bright stars tonight telling stories. The stars always look so much brighter and bigger when you're out in country like this. Seems like we are just closer than when at home. Both Ned and I fell into the river today. The joke was on us. Need to watch my step.

"Eighth Day. The Salmon seems more narrow and the rapids higher. Some were six and ten feet. Some are afraid to go through Porcupine Rapids in the morning so I imagine we'll carry the boats and baggage around. High rock mountains are all around us.

"Final Day. Went through Redside and Great River rapids. Very high and exciting. Hated that this was our last day of going down, down, down the Salmon. We reached the junction of Middlefork and Salmon rivers at 2:00 p.m., and then unpacked and deflated the rafts. Drove over a rough road to Challis and then on to spend the night here at Jack's brother's home on Bear Valley Creek near Mackay. We'll return to Salt Lake City tomorrow and I'll be taking the bus for Seattle and then a plane for Sitka. Thank God for the many blessings of this wonderful trip. I hardly feel that I deserve to enjoy His beautiful handiwork on these incredible landscapes. Remember to be thankful. Go in His way."

Gracie recalled that she had a premonition of some kind about what turned out to be her last wild river trip. It was on the Colorado River in May of 1962.

"I was exhausted from overwork at the hospital and at home. I was substituting for a sick co-worker at Blount Memorial and hadn't had a day off in almost three weeks. I was trying to move some bushes in my fenced-in yard at the trailer park. I spent the first day of my vacation at Ruth's, and her husband, George, usually not one to comment on another's plans, had said, 'Gracie, those are awful dangerous trips you take. You might not get back.' Of course, I didn't pay any attention to him.

"Although I knew that I was tired and not in my usual high spirits before a river rat trip, I couldn't forget that Jack had written that by the next summer much of the part of the Colorado that we were going to run—350 miles in the Grand Canyon—would be controlled as the result of the Glen Canyon Dam.

"Jack and Don had always said it was the prettiest part of the river. So I flew to Phoenix and from there took a small plane to a ranch in the Grand Canyon, where I joined Jack and Don and 12 other people.

"All 15 of us were to go in five boats—two owned and piloted by physicians. Don and Jack each piloted a boat, and I had always ridden with one of them. But by the time I arrived one physician's woman friend had asked to ride with the guides, saying that her date was too reckless on the rapids. Don was in a spot with the woman asking to ride with him, so I agreed to help out and ride with the doctor.

"I became very alarmed at the way the doctor shot a couple of rapids and started to get out of the boat and walk around a rapid—Lava Rapid near Phantom's Ranch—that was coming up. But I hesitated to do that, realizing that the doctor would think I didn't have confidence in him. I should have followed my intuition.

Two days after this picture was shot on the Colorado River in the Grand Canyon in July of 1962, Gracie broke her back in a rapid-shooting accident. She struggled for four days with the injury to get out of the canyon and reach medical treatment.

"Each of the boats shot Lava Rapids separately, with the forerunners waiting until all were through. Someone later sent me a picture of us coming through, and we were seven to 10 feet above the water. I was holding to the outside of the boat and underneath the windshield and bracing with my feet. When we hit, it seemed like a sharp knife was cutting through my back. My glasses and cap flew off, but I didn't lose them because I had tied them to my shirt by shoestrings.

"The pain was so great I had to lie down flat in the bottom of the boat...sitting was impossible. We soon stopped at the only place en route that we got supplies, and another doctor in our party gave me a shot of Demerol and I lay in the sand, flat on my stomach, the only way I am usually comfortable when lying down.

"It was very painful for me to tie my shoe or do anything for myself, but being accustomed to living alone I wouldn't ask anyone for help. I lay on the sand while they lowered supplies from the top of the canyon wall on a rope. We had two more days to travel before reaching Lake Mead, the end of our trip. There was no way out...I think it would have been impossible to hoist me up over the high canyon wall by rope, although I think they did discuss that.

"The doctor's boat was the only one big enough for me to lie prone on the floor...so I had to go with him. When we stopped the only way I could bear to move was by pressing the injured part of my back at my waistline with my fingers, holding tight, while I walked very erectly. Demerol and sleeping pills kept me from tensing up too much, but I was never free of pain completely."

The situation worsened dramatically for the entire party the next day. Don's boat broke down, and Jack had to help him try to make repairs. It was decided that Gracie would go ahead with the physicians so that she could be taken to a hospital.

"I almost cried telling Jack and Don goodbye, but I managed to hold back the tears because I knew they felt so badly about everything," she recalled sadly.

"I feared that I would never see them again. And I didn't."

"The two physicians piloted their boats into Lake Meade, while the guides and their passengers remained behind," said Gracie. "The lake waters were whipped by a high wind, making the waves choppy. I felt every one in my back. It grew dark and the two boats became separated, and I longed so much for the calm and knowledge that Jack and Don had exhibited on my six other river trips. Now our boat was leaking and we had to pull ashore for the night.

"Although we had no bedding and food (they were with the guides), we somehow survived until morning. Fortunately, the leak was a slow one and they were able to keep the water dipped out. I just lay on the floor with only the thickness of a mattress holding me above water as we limped into port."

The other physician and his party had already arrived, also hungry and exhausted but without a leak in their boat. Gracie lay on her stomach in the back of a station wagon while one of the men drove her to Las Vegas.

"I was hurting terribly but didn't want to go in the hospital out there because I would have no family close by. So I checked into a motel and tried to rest, but couldn't because of the pain. Finally, at 1:00 a.m. on Monday I caught a flight to Atlanta by way of Louisiana. I telephoned Ruth from Atlanta to meet me in Knoxville.

"When I got off the plane and saw her, I finally broke down and started crying. It was Monday afternoon, and I had hurt my back on Friday. They X-rayed me at Blount Memorial Hospital, and the doctor's diagnosis was fractured and compressed vertebra. The original plan was to operate, but they actually didn't...I guess because I began to improve, lying on a board."

After six weeks of that in the hospital, Gracie was released to go home, with orders to wear a brace from hips to neck for nine months when not lying down. Ruth came over to help some at first, and as time went by Eula Fry began to suggest that Gracie try a little walking. It didn't take much to get her interested in that, so soon she was walking around the trailer park and then on the adjoining railroad tracks, a spur seldom traveled by trains.

Eula took her up to the Sugarland Trail near Fighting Creek Gap, a trail usually considered easy. But Gracie soon learned that you naturally bend your body backward when walking downgrade and the reverse for going up. Since she had to walk erect in the brace, it proved a slow process.

"Eula kept encouraging me, and I walked about a mile and had lunch. Eventually she insisted on trying a hike on the Appalachian Trail from Newfound Gap. I got so carried away at being out in the balsam forest again that we almost went too far...I kept imagining how things might be up on Le Conte that day," Gracie recalled.

She used up all of her sick leave at Blount Memorial, and was then given leave without pay. But the doctors had ordered her to wear the brace for nine full months, and there seemed no way to carry out her nursing duties without bending, an impossible procedure in the orthopaedic appliance.

"Well, I finally had to retire. They needed to fill the position. The Maryville doctor had told me that I was most fortunate not to have been hurt worse, and I've realized that I could have been paralyzed from the neck down. When we can't see ahead, God can see. Perhaps He wanted me to quit the river trips and to also quit working at the hospital. It was 1962, and I would be 71 in October. I had been nursing for 30 years in spite of my late start."

Her diary entry summed it up: "I finally retired from Blount Memorial today. It's 30 years since I started nursing in Kansas. As a nurse I almost always finished each day feeling that I had done some good for somebody. The work was repetitive but the people were all different, and that was the most important part of all. I feel that it was truly God's work and thank Him for giving me all those opportunities to help folks along the way. Will I ever get used to not wearing white?"

Recalling her retirement, Gracie said, "The hardest part was going back to the hospital to pick up my uniforms and caps. I used to dress for work at Blount Memorial, since they did our white cotton uniforms with the hospital laundry.

Somehow I got through that final uniform checkout, and I would go back occasionally to visit with the nurses on the afternoon shift, walking to and from in my brace."

Talking about living on Social Security is one thing, but actually doing it is a different matter. She had some savings, but she didn't want to go into that. She had no pension except Social Security. Gracie worried some about finances, as do most persons reaching retirement, but she was proud of her thrifty Scotch ways. She had spent money on vacations far more liberally than some people through the years, but she easily made up for it the rest of the time, living in the small trailer and doing all laundry in the washhouse next door.

Finding ways to save money became critical in the fabric of her daily life. For example, she never purchased plastic wrap or wax paper, always saving wrappings from bread and similarly packaged food. She found the backs of envelopes adequate for her voluminous notes on nature. For years she carried a few envelopes from mail addressed to her along to Le Conte. When other guests asked for her address, she had only to produce a used envelope with ready-made information.

Never one to spend much money on clothes, she usually kept only two or three nice dresses for church and such occasions. With her trim figure, she could find good buys on clothes at rummage sales. Her entertainment had always been hiking, bus trips, and church.

Gracie said that the importance of wasting nothing in the form of material things was stressed in the McNicol home as she grew into adulthood. "My father, James McNicol, was born in Glasgow in 1848, and the family moved to the United States in 1858. It would have been impossible for them to immigrate and then prosper in this country if they hadn't saved every way they could.

"Mother was Pennsylvania Dutch—her name was Henrietta Holderman—and she was as accustomed to 'making do' with little, as was my father. If they hadn't managed and saved the way they did, we children wouldn't have been able

would drive by and suggest that they go up into the Smokies to walk a bit on one of the trails off Highway 441. They'd sometimes stop at Fighting Creek Gap on a clear day and gaze at Le Conte's lofty heights, even more splendid than usual in the fall with touches of gold and red on lower slopes. A faint purple haze around the peaks hinted of the coming winter.

The two women took the Alum Cave Bluffs Trail to Gracie's Pulpit a couple of times in September, with the nurse repeating her favorite Bible verse with fervor as she gazed at the top of the mountain: "I will lift up mine eyes unto the hills, from whence cometh my help. My help cometh from the Lord...."

With brace intact, Gracie made it alone all the way to the top of Le Conte to celebrate her 71st birthday. The lodge staff staged a big celebration with cake and all the trimmings.

Throughout the winter she continued to walk around the trailer park and downtown Maryville, enjoying longer treks in the mountains with Eula when her friend could schedule them. She had become accustomed to the brace by the time it was removed in the spring of 1963. With her back fully recovered from the rapids shooting injury, she looked forward to glimpsing the first bloom of trailing arbutus on Bullhead Trail.

Grace McNichol traveled to Franklin, North Carolina, in May 1975 to hear Father Morgan preach in his Episcopal chapel. Here they discuss the service on the porch of the chapel.

The Competition

During the early days (1950s) a friendly competition began to emerge between Gracie and another frequent hiker to the lodge atop Mount Le Conte: Rev. A. Rufus Morgan, a retired Episcopal priest living in Franklin, North Carolina.

Herrick Brown and his wife, Myrtle, had begun operating the lodge in 1960, purchasing the interests of the Huffs when Pauline retired at the end of the 1959 season. Like the Huffs, the Browns obtained a franchise from the National Park Service to run the mountain hostel. Herrick recalled that the Reverend Morgan had been hiking the Southern mountains for most of his life and had been climbing Le Conte to stay in the lodge as long as anyone could remember.

"He would come 10 or 11 times a year usually. Former parishioners and friends would come up with him when they could manage to be in the area for two or three days. He usually came on Wednesdays and Gracie on Mondays. As it became known that they had made more trips up the mountain than anyone but lodge personnel, a bit of competition began to develop," Herrick recalled, "Gracie was coming twice a month or more."

Herrick, or "Brownie," as Gracie and other longtime hikers came to call him, thinks the priest missed a year about the time Gracie was having trouble with her back. He had vision problems and possibly surgery, Herrick said.

Both of the "friendly competitors" were born in October, with Father Morgan celebrating his 75th birthday in 1960 and Gracie marking her 69th. They liked to observe their birthdays at the lodge on Le Conte. By the end of 1960, the priest was listing 39 hikes up the mountain and Gracie 52.

During the Browns' 14 years as operators of the lodge, a 90-year-old man from Maryville was the oldest person to make the climb and their 3-year-old daughter, Barbara, was the youngest.

Gracie did not remember the year she first met the Reverend Morgan at the lodge, but she remembered the occasion. Following dinner she and other guests had gone to Cliff Top to await the sunset. It was a clear evening with visibility ranging over hundreds of square miles to the west.

The sun seemed to hang still as the guests talked softly in the glow, sitting on rocks amid the Carolina rhododendron and sand myrtle, a glossy-leaf evergreen. The hikers included the priest and some friends and a group of members of the cast of *Unto These Hills*. It was a Monday, the only non-performance night of the week for them.

"Just as the bottom edge of the sun began to sink below the horizon, a beautiful young woman who had separated herself from the group and was standing alone on a big rock began to sing "Indian Love Call."

"It was so beautiful it seemed like a dream, and I don't think anyone said a word. The sun disappeared, leaving only a glow in the clouds; she finished the song and returned to us. The young actors encouraged everyone to join hands, and we sang 'Amazing Grace' and 'Go Tell It on the Mountain.' It was a very moving experience," Gracie remembered. "I wiped tears from my eyes as I walked back to the lodge in the darkness."

She did not actually meet Father Morgan until she returned to the lodge and learned she and a single woman in his party had been assigned a bedroom behind the fireplace in one of the four-room cabins.

"He's just a wonderful person," said Gracie. "He loves the mountains and the hiking and can remember all sorts of tales about the Smokies and Le Conte.

"Once when talking with him I looked at the sky and said

Rev. Rufus Morgan of Franklin, North Carolina, and Gracie competed for the title of "most trips up Le Conte." At this meeting on the mountaintop in April 1976, Father Morgan counted 161 trips and Gracie 177.

'Evening star and one clear call for me.' He repeated the remainder of Tennyson's entire poem without hesitation. And I never heard anyone mention a portion of the Bible to him that he could not recite, word for word, even Revelations."

Gracie enjoyed a trip to Franklin, North Carolina, with Emily Wessel of Newburgh, Indiana, whom she met at the Wildflower Pilgrimage in Gatlinburg, and the two visited Father Morgan's church. Although retired, he still had services in a tiny chapel that featured a window behind the altar through which the congregation could view birds and flowers and the distant mountains.

"The service was even more sacred with the beauty of the Lord for us to see," observed Gracie.

She said Father Morgan, wearing a red-checked shirt and carrying a pack, usually came up one of the five trails leading to Le Conte's summit accompanied by five to fifteen friends. Often he came up with members of the Nantahala Hiking Club. "He enjoys hiking so much that it just makes people want to join in," she said.

Both she and the priest would write the number of each particular trip opposite their names when they signed in the register. Guests would sometimes check to see the status of their "race" for the most trips to the lodge. By the end of 1965 Father Morgan was listing 66 and Gracie 122. The gap was soon to narrow.

Standing at Fighting Creek Gap, Gracie enjoys a view of three-peaked Mount Le Conte on a fall morning before starting her ascent up the mountain by horse.

Lost on Cole Creek

Gracie's trip diaries always note which trail was taken on ascent, destinations on walks atop Le Conte, and which trail was followed on descent. Her summary for 1966 listed a total of 18 trips: eight up Alum Cave, 10 up Boulevard, 15 down Bullhead, one down Trillium Gap, one down Rainbow Falls, and one down Cole Creek. Cole Creek courses down the mountain's western slope and is not a trail. That descent is the one time in all her Le Conte trips that the nurse failed to follow the old hiking adage with which she heartily agrees: "Stay on the trail at all times."

Myrtle Brown had a few free hours one August afternoon and suggested that she and her frequent guest take a walk through the forest on the western side of Le Conte between Alum Cave and Bullhead trails to see a giant Fraser balsam fir tree said to be of record size.

Gracie accepted eagerly, having come to treasure any time walking on the mountaintop with lodge operators because they knew so many delightful secrets about unusual plants, special places, and splendid vistas. The Browns, like the Huffs before them, had little spare time during the season because they were usually booked solid, doing some repairs, gathering and chopping wood, and occasionally erecting new buildings—all of that in addition to serving guests.

Myrtle was generally on hand in the summer to supervise meal preparation and serving for guests, and she did all of the cooking for the crew.

The two women left the lodge at 2:30 p.m. and walked to the fir tree, marveling at its eight-foot circumference. They put their arms around it and touched hands.

Leaving the tree, they cut through the forest in what they thought was a northerly direction, expecting to come out on the Bullhead trail and return to the lodge. Myrtle needed to begin preparation of dinner at 4:00 o'clock. Some 50 guests were expected that evening.

"It was my mistake, I think," said Gracie. "I think I must have borne too much to the left, or south. It was cloudy and we could not get our bearings. Finally realizing that we could not find the way to Bullhead Trail, we decided to try another hiking adage: 'If you get lost, follow a stream.'"

They were above Cole Creek, although not sure of that at the time, and began to follow dry stream beds in the direction of what they assumed would be a creek with running water. The trails on Le Conte, like most in the national park, are about a yard wide and well-maintained. Occasionally trails round sheer bluffs where the hiker must hold onto a cable, but usually it's a smooth, albeit narrow pathway.

The two women soon learned what the original blazers of those trails had encountered: a virtual jungle of rhododendron and laurel growing amid a tumble of boulders broken loose through thousands of years of erosion. Decaying trunks of fallen trees nourished the lush plant life and acted as traps for the feet of hikers. The endless greenery of the mountainside, so beautiful when viewed from the developed trails, was almost impossible to penetrate in actual contact.

"We had to climb over or under rotting, fallen trees and we would think we had a firm foothold, only to have our weight push our feet down into leaf-covered crevices between rocks and trunks of dead trees. Sometimes we had to actually scoot over the tops of rhododendron because there was no way to go through a tangle. All the stories I'd heard about Huggins' Hell came back to me as I tried to keep up with Myrtle," Gracie remembered.

The lodge operator was middle-aged, and Gracie was 74 years old. The two vowed not to get separated, which was very difficult in the tangle. "If she got a few paces ahead, she'd wait for me, and I'd do the same for her."

Having found Cole Creek, the women stayed away from its banks, thinking it would be harder descending where undergrowth might be thicker and rocks slick.

After a time they heard someone yelling, and they answered over and over, but to no avail. They were to learn later that Brownie had guessed they had taken a wrong turn and had sent a young staff member named Gene Johnson to find them. He came down the banks of the creek and was unable to hear their answering calls because he was too close to the noisy, rushing water.

Gracie fell into a leaf-covered hole in a boulder and cut her shin. Myrtle bandaged it with her handkerchief, which stopped the bleeding. But thereafter Gracie found lifting her leg was even harder.

"From time to time we still heard someone calling, but we couldn't tell which direction the voice was coming from. So we decided the only thing we could do was to keep going down in the general direction of the stream, hoping to come out on the transmountain highway, U.S. 441," Gracie said.

"When you're lost like that, everything looks the same... especially when it began to grow dusky as sunset time drew near. Myrtle was wearing a green blouse with white stripes, and finally I could see only the white stripes in the dusk. For a while I was just following the stripes.

"Suddenly, we heard horns blowing and figured we were nearing the road and, sure enough, we came out on the highway at Cove Branch near the loop. Two park service patrol cars were there, and they were trying to decide whether to start up the creek looking for us. It was eight o'clock and we'd left the lodge six and one-half hours earlier. We learned that it was four miles straight down the mountain, but don't know how far we came following the stream.

"As we were talking to the rangers, Gene Johnson came out of the tangle of laurel and we learned that he never heard us hollering, probably because of the noise of the water.

"There are some big waterfalls on Cole Creek, and he

jumped from rock to rock in places. I was so thankful that he was not hurt.

"Myrtle insisted that I go to the doctor and see if my shinbone was cracked. It wasn't, but an infection developed and I had to go to the hospital for a few days to recuperate. I was pretty disgusted with myself for having gone off trail and put everyone to so much trouble."

She made no entry in her diary that night, but the next day she wrote: "Lord, you delivered me out of the fiery furnace. I trusted in you and you led the way through that fearful confusion. I will try to be more responsible in my actions. Thank you for bringing Gene Johnson safely out of there."

Gracie pointed out that several persons have become lost in the years she's been hiking in the Smokies, and two of them have never been found. In one case a seven-year-old boy hiking with his family disappeared on Gregory Bald in 1969, and a few years later a teenage girl vanished not too far away, near Clingman's Dome.

Gracie's near desperate struggle through the tangled growth convinced her that leaving the trail could easily be a life-threatening move. "All the bushes and trees which you can view from the trail and enjoy as they wave in the wind and sunlight, become hateful obstacles when you have to go through them. I don't advise it for anyone. And from nature's point of view, it probably does a lot of harm for people to try to hike off the trails, stepping on delicate plants," Gracie pointed out.

However, she said that she wouldn't take anything for the experience on Cole Creek because it was so interesting to see different flowers, ferns, and moss—moss several inches thick growing like a huge rug in many places. Once, she said, she spotted a clump of flowers in a sunny place—turtleheads, bee balm and cohosh—and stopped to enjoy them. Myrtle grew impatient, feeling it was not the time to study flowers, a hobby she usually enjoyed, according to Gracie.

Friends at the lodge teased Gracie during the summer of 1966, saying she'd just gone down Cole Creek to have a "mountain tale" to match some of those told by her mountain-climbing competitor, Father Morgan. Their tallies were 72 trips for him and 140 for her at the end of the season that year.

Father Morgan, always an amicable rival, was soon to begin pointing out that Gracie's method of ascent had changed from his and therefore should perhaps be considered differently. He would be referring to the outcome of a dire struggle that Gracie faced during 1967.

During three decades, Gracie hiked on all of the many trails, both short and long, in Great Smoky Mountains National Park. Here she prepares for a quick jaunt to Laurel Falls, one of the self-guided nature trails.

Gracie and Jean Feldman of Chapel Hill, North Carolina, met at Myrtle Point at sunrise and stayed there all day sunning on the rocks.

Celebrating her 92nd birthday at the lodge on October 1, 1983, Gracie is joined by nephews Robert Dougherty (left) and Austin (Doc) Williams of Washington, D.C.

Life Almost Slipped Away

Gracie had been able to remove her back brace by April of 1963 and for the next four years had made up for the hiking time lost during the summer of '62. The 18 trips up Le Conte during 1966 had been made without special effort except for the Cole Creek incident. She once hiked the eight-mile Boulevard Trail in three and one-half hours with Carolyn Brown, the 13-year-old daughter of the lodge operators.

She was also attending the annual wildflower pilgrimages in April, when thousands come to Gatlinburg's auditorium to study wildflowers on display and then go into the surrounding mountains to find them blooming alongside trails and roads. Gracie was studying her own copy of *Great Smoky Mountain Wildflowers* by Campbell, Hutson, and Sharp and leafing through tree identification books to find a tree seen on her latest hike on Le Conte.

The mountain is considered to have almost as many species of trees as are found in all of Europe. Its virgin forests were spared from the ravages of lumbering only by a hairbreadth when they were included in the area designated a national park by the United States government in 1935.

The world's largest hemlock tree—with a 20-foot girth—was growing on Le Conte in the 1960s, as were record specimens of yellow buckeye, mountain maple, and American mountain ash. The Fraser balsam fir west of the lodge which Gracie and Myrtle had walked out to see sets a world record with its eight-foot circumference.

Gracie marveled at the deciduous trees from their earliest, tissuey shoots in the spring to their yellow-, red-, and brown-colored coats in October.

She recalled: "People would say, 'Don't you get tired of going to the same place over and over and seeing the same things?' But I told them that it's different every trip, changing from day to day and month to month. Going down Bullhead on a May day you can see more than 60 wildflowers and trees blooming. On that same trail in August you'd see at least half that number of different flowers in bloom along with mushrooms of many colors, if the humidity is right."

There is a special serenity and feeling of the continuity of life when walking Le Conte trails in virgin forests. Such forests are rare because of heavy timbering by the pioneers. You know that some of the trees overhead stood sentinel in those same spots during the American Revolution.

Flowering trees located at various elevations include the redbud and the white dogwood, which wave their lacy blooms in April and May, the sourwood and black locust, which bloom in summer, and, of course, the mighty tulip tree, known in the Smokies as yellow poplar. Its tulip-shaped blooms of orange and green open in late spring. Honeybees cover the sourwood, locust, and poplar.

After retiring, Gracie was able to study more about the abundant plant life that greeted her on every hand as she walked the trails of her vast mountain garden. She sometimes climbed to the lodge two or three times a month, when finances would permit.

Although most persons make reservations far ahead—the lodge even then was booked solid for months—the Browns could usually work Gracie into a cabin or lodge bedroom with another single woman on a few days' notice. She was always willing to take the top bunk or a cot or whatever was available. Once she slept in the dining room on a foldaway bed.

Eula had returned to work after her son got older, and Gracie made almost all of her trips to the mountains by bus during 1965 and 1966, going the old 65-mile route via Knoxville and Sevierville.

The next major crisis in Gracie's life began in January of 1967, her 76th year, although she didn't realize it at the time: "Having been outside every minute I could during the summer and fall, I was working almost desperately around the trailer trying to take care of all the housework and general maintenance I'd neglected. My chest began to hurt, and I kept swinging my arms around to take the pain out with exercise. It was the worse thing I could have done."

On January 26 Gracie caught the bus as usual for Sunday services at the Tabernacle Baptist Church in Knoxville, which she had begun attending four years previously after hearing the preacher on the radio. "He sounded like the Evangelical ministers of my childhood," she explained.

As her Sunday school class was ending, Gracie recalled that she began to feel "smothery" and went to ask the bus driver (the church bus carried her to and from the Greyhound bus station) to take her to a vacant classroom to rest until he was ready to leave after worship services. The driver apparently became alarmed and summoned some women and the assistant pastor.

"I lay down, but couldn't get comfortable. I was desperately cold and I felt myself slipping away. I tried to hold on...to listen to what they were saying...to think...to tell them I was so cold...but I couldn't do it...I couldn't hold on...I knew that I was slipping away," she remembered, clasping her hands and pausing for a moment.

Gracie awoke about six o'clock that evening at Knoxville's Presbyterian Hospital to learn that she had suffered a stroke. Movement caused severe pain, especially above the waist, she said. The top of her head hurt terribly.

"But I was not paralyzed, and I was so grateful for that. I was shocked that I had suffered a stroke and I guess, looking back, ashamed of having one, feeling somehow disgraced. I don't know why I felt that way exactly, but it was a long time before I told anyone that it was a stroke. But it must have been obvious that I was sick for some reason.

"My sister Ruth was spending some time in Arizona that year and so I really didn't have any family to help much. But as has happened so often in my life, someone came along when I needed them most. The assistant pastor took me home six days after the stroke, and then the landlord and a neighbor, a Mason who was a very kind man, helped me by doing my grocery shopping. I have oil heat in the trailer and so it was no problem."

Although a 29-foot mobile home is small, Gracie found taking even a few steps from bedroom to kitchen painful at first. The doctors had told her the pain was caused by poor circulation. Hospital tests had shown a high level of cholesterol.

"To lower the level and thereby reduce the danger of another stroke, they told me to eat a low-fat diet and avoid high cholesterol foods entirely.

"I had bossed a lot of people in my times as a nurse, so I decided to boss myself and try to improve my health. I started avoiding fatty foods and canned foods with their additives, buying fresh vegetables and cooking them without fat. Before long I had come to like rye bread, peanut butter, margarine, raisins, vegetables, and fruit," she laughed.

Having drunk whole milk all her life, she switched to skim. Avoiding alcoholic beverages was no problem, because she had never tasted the substance. Waiting on drunks as a nurse had cured her of any desire in that direction. She had never smoked tobacco, either.

Planning her meals very carefully and still managing to stay within her strict budget, she made lists and the neighbor kindly shopped for the best prices. Leaving nothing to chance, she even checked to make sure she was taking a few more steps each day than the day before. She kept written notes on the number of steps taken at any time during the day so that she could look back and be sure to increase them.

"That was the longest February of my life since the two years that I was bedridden, and remembering how it was to be unable to get up, I pushed myself to walk around the trailer. Each day I went a few steps further and gradually walked out on my little porch. Then I walked the 10 or 15 feet to my front gate. Sometimes my breath would become labored after only five or six steps on level ground. So I learned to just stop and rest a few seconds," she explained.

Gracie enlarged her itinerary throughout the month of March, first walking just to the washhouse, then to a neighbor's house on the other side. Later she walked to the creek to see if any wildflowers were showing...and found a violet.

"I had pains above my waist every day," she remembered, "but I knew I had to keep moving. I had always walked my way back to health when things looked darkest."

Staying within sight of the trailer park during March, she was walking on the railroad tracks a little by the end of the month. Seeing dandelions and wild geraniums blooming alongside the ties increased her longing to attend the wildflower pilgrimage, which was to be held the last week of April at the Gatlinburg Auditorium.

As the time for the pilgrimage approached, she decided to just go up to the motel across from the auditorium where she had stayed for several years. The auditorium would be no greater distance to walk than the railroad tracks, she reasoned.

Laundering her clothes one or two items a day for more than a week, Gracie was finally ready when the pilgrimage opening date arrived. She took a taxicab to the bus station in Maryville and rode to Knoxville to catch the transmountain bus going through Gatlinburg. Thinking she would not be physically or financially able to go outside the motel to eat, she carried enough peanut butter and raisin sandwiches, carrots, apples, powdered milk, and decaffeinated coffee to last the whole time. The room had an electric pot to make coffee.

"I went to bed to rest as soon as I arrived at the motel and promised to make myself take it easy the three days," she said, "but when I saw all of the wildflowers sparkling on the tables in the auditorium the next day, I so longed to see them growing along the roadsides and on the trails."

She went along when cars arrived to take wildflower viewers into the mountains. "I knew I mustn't walk any because it would be too taxing...so I just stood outside the car while the other passengers walked down side trails to get better views. Some flowers were right beside the road and I was so thankful to be able to see them. Patches of pure white bloodroot sparkled in the sun, and when I saw whole banks covered with the pinkish haze of spring beauty, I knew that the new season had come. The white phacelia looked like banks of snow in Smokemont."

And from several locations along the road, when the winds blew the mists of April away, Gracie caught glimpses of Mount Le Conte, distant and beautiful, towering over Gatlinburg, its peaks capped in snow one morning. She knew the trailing arbutus would be blooming in clusters of pink and white beside Bullhead Trail, their fragrance wafting up the pathway, beckoning the hiker. She also knew that Herrick Brown had begun operating the lodge for the season in late March. The couple had a house in Gatlinburg where they lived in winter, and Myrtle usually stayed there most of the time while their three children were attending area schools.

"The Browns had telephoned to say they were expecting me during the 1967 season, and I had promised to keep walking until I built up to the Mount Le Conte climb," remembered Gracie.

Back home after the pilgrimage, her longing for the mountain became almost unbearable when the warm breezes began to blow in the shiny, new maple leaves at Shady Grove Trailer Park. If she took the transmountain bus, she would have seven hours on the Alum Cave Bluffs Trail before time to catch the return bus. With courage high on a bright day in early May, she telephoned a taxi to take her to the bus station to begin the two and one-half hour ride to the Alum Cave Bluffs Trail head beside U.S. Highway 441.

"I worried some about doing that, but decided that if I got to feeling poorly, I would just sit beside the highway until the Knoxville-bound bus came in the afternoon."

Getting off the bus and starting along the trail early in the morning just like old times brought back a flood of memories.

"Having my feet on Le Conte soil was like magic, but I had

to stop every ten steps or so to rest, if going upward. I didn't go very far...just walked until I could no longer hear cars on the highway. I sat down on a log beside Alum Cave Creek, and it was so soothing to listen to the water.

"The sunlight came down in slanting rays through the hemlocks, and the birds were singing. It was so peaceful and beautiful...so perfect in every way. God had been so good to permit me to be there."

She was to return several times in May as a passenger on the transmountain bus, going a little higher each time. The rhododendron began to bloom in late May near the bottom of the trail, and she knew that soon the groves around Gracie's Pulpit three miles higher would look like wedding bowers.

Ruth had come home from Arizona, and she and her son, Robert, and her daugher, Connie, and Ruth's four grandchildren invited Gracie on a surprise outing in late May: walk with them up the Alum Cave Bluffs Trail as far as she felt like going. Since the Doughertys were apparently going to get a late start, Gracie suggested that she ride the bus as usual and start hiking, with the family to hike until they caught up with her.

"I had my notepad with me and kept leaving them notes all along the way, putting bits of paper in obvious places, weighted with rocks. It rained and I wondered what they would do, but I kept pushing ahead...I wanted to get to Gracie's Pulpit and see Mount Le Conte. I had not dared go that high by myself since the stroke," Gracie remembered.

"I got over this dirty, filthy thing," she wrote on the note left at Alum Cave, which had never won her heart although many enjoy viewing the effects of the erosion which has produced the giant overhanging shelf.

Resting several times as she climbed the very steep grade at the bluff, she looked down the trail but saw no sign of the Doughterys. Gracie's Pulpit was only about a half mile around the ridge. She pushed on, albeit resting every few yards.

Rounding a long curve in the trail, she saw Gracie's Pulpit just ahead. The "window" through the forested trailside showed Cliff Top, the western peak of Le Conte, many shades of green amid the rocks. Clouds from the recent shower were drifting at lower elevations, but the sun was shining on top. It was lunchtime, and Gracie knew that Brownie and Myrtle and the staff would be eating in the dining room, looking down at Knoxville and Douglas Lake in the Tennessee Valley.

"I always thank God for my blessings when I reach the pulpit," said Gracie, "and on that day I was so grateful to have been able to walk that far again, considering the great distance my front gate had seemed only four months before."

Her notepad for the trip bore this inscription: "Breathe on me breath of God. Fill me with life anew that I may love what thou dost love...and do what Thou wouldst do. In Jesus name I pray."

She sat down to eat a sandwich, only to be joined by great nephew Johnny Dougherty, then about age 14, who reported that the rest of the family had gone back to Arch Rock for shelter when the shower started.

Recounting the experience to her doctor the next week, Gracie hoped that he would say she could hike all the way to the top of Le Conte. He wouldn't hear of it, saying the experience would be too exhausting, but he did sanction a plan suggested a few weeks earlier by the Browns: making the trip on horseback.

In those days and until the 1970s, all food and supplies were brought up to the lodge by horses traveling on the Rainbow Falls or Trillium Gap trails. Several guests usually came up on horses each day, rented at two riding stables located near the foot of the mountain. It was Myrtle Brown's idea that Gracie should take the bus to her house on Monday, rest and stay overnight, and ascend the mountain on Tuesday morning with the packhorses.

Arrangements were made with Smoky Mountain Hiking Stables for a ride up on May 30. Except for a couple of visits to dude ranches in the West, Gracie had ridden little since the days when the McNicol children had "climbed all over old Nell" at the nursery. "I worried a little about getting on and off, but the men at the stable assured me by telephone that they would see that I had no trouble," Gracie said.

After a restful night at the Brown home in Gatlinburg, Brownie drove Gracie to the Rainbow Falls Trail head in Cherokee Orchard and began to hike up to the lodge himself following the telephone line which ran nearby.

Gracie was delighted when Hugh Carter appeared with the horses, leading a reliable 22-year-old gelding named Ben for her to ride.

Hugh calmed her fears about getting on the horse by joking that it was a pleasure to help 111-pound Gracie into the saddle after some of the rotund passengers he'd had the previous week. "I know one woman weighed 200 pounds," he said.

Hugh gave Gracie some tips on keeping toes pointed outward and taking her feet out of the stirrups occasionally to avoid leg cramps. As the horses began the 4,100-foot climb, Gracie realized that the horse wasn't Old Nell and the steep grade bore no resemblance to the plains of Kansas or even

Gracie and a young couple take a break on Rocky Spur on the Rainbow Falls Trail. The top of Mount Le Conte and a panoramic view many be seen from this outcropping, which is surrounded by sand myrtle.

Marvin McCarter of McCarter's Stables welcomes Gracie as he starts to lead a group up Rainbow Falls to Mount Le Conte in November 1977, her 200th-trip year.

the dude ranches. The horse was trained to keep up with the mount ahead, and when he felt that he was getting behind, he'd start trotting. Gracie remembered to stand up in the stirrups, and it spared her derriere.

The Rainbow Falls Trail has few level stretches, unlike some other trails that follow contour lines more. Gracie tried to lean forward a little to make her weight easier on the horse for the almost constant upward pull, and she gave Ben full rein, deciding that the horse was the veteran on that trail and would make better decisions than she. Soon they encountered stretches on ledges falling away 50 to 100 feet and more, straight down. The trail was rock strewn in many places, and she tried hard not to think of what could happen if the horse stumbled.

"And sometimes they did stumble, but we usually didn't let them trot in such places, reining in at those times," Gracie explained.

Reaching Rainbow Falls, Hugh suggested that the small party dismount and take a break. Gracie declined to dismount, not wanting to put Hugh to the trouble, but she took advantage of the time to take both feet out of the stirrups and swing them around and to eat a sandwich. Remembering Old Nell's preferences, she had brought along an apple for the horse, who turned his head to gaze momentarily into her eyes with an expression of gratitude.

Rainbow Falls is located about three and one-half miles up on the 6.75-mile trail to Le Conte and has traditionally been a favorite hike for visitors to the Smokies. Crystal clear water ran down the rocks and fell in long streams that day because May is a month of heavy rainfall in the Smokies.

Gracie was delighted to see trilliums, red-berried elder, galax, wood sorrel, foamflower, mountain laurel blooms, and many violets along the trail. Her wildflowers-in-bloom count reached 26 that day. She knew that the witch-hobble bushes would be blooming on Le Conte and felt a tingle of excitement in her stomach at the thought of seeing their white clusters once again.

Climbing above Rainbow Falls, the horses picked their ways carefully through rocks and some ruts in the trail, and Gracie finally became accustomed to looking straight down the mountainside when the trail ran along a ledge. Within three hours they reached Rocky Spur, a platform overlooking hundreds of miles of lower mountains, foothills, and flatlands to the north and northeast. Looking upward and southwesterly, they saw the top of Le Conte for the first time that day. Gracie said that her heart leaped at the sight, "but I tried to sit still on my horse in that place." It was clear on top, and she would be spending two nights, having plenty of time to rest before the stable would send a horse and guide for her on the third day.

The party rode to the hitching post at the lodge 30 minutes later, and Brownie was waiting to greet them. "It was just like coming home to see all the staff again...several of the nice young people had returned from the year before," she recalled with a smile.

The staff had her room ready in the old lodge, but before retiring for a nap she ate a sandwich and wrote in her notebook: "My 142nd trip, first by horse in 13 years of climbing the mountain. God is so good to me."

The fragrance of balsam that pervades the air at the lodge most of the time was like a tonic, and she napped and walked around a little before dinner. She was her usual self at mealtime, sharing the excitement of the ascent with people at her table who had come from several states. But she decided against trying to walk to Cliff Top or Myrtle Point to see the sunset. "I just stood outside and watched the light dim from gold to dusk to black in the Tennessee Valley. It was such a joy to return to the four-room lodge and sit around the fire telling mountain tales," remembered Gracie.

The fire was welcome because the temperature was in the 50s. Since the lodge's beginning in 1925, wood for fires had been cut from balsam trees blown down during storms, a practice that would be stopped by the Park Service in the 1970s.

The most modern convenience at the lodge was the telephone, put in by the Huffs, who had the wire strung through the forest near the Rainbow Falls Trail. The winds would blow the line around and break it, and the staff would have to find the trouble spot and patch the strands. Keeping the phone line in operation provided many lively tales that were passed down through the years from staff member to staff member.

Instead of her usual walk to the overlook points at Myrtle Point and Cliff Top, Gracie strolled only short distances from the lodge the next day, resting frequently on fallen trees and rocks, while admiring sweet white violets, witch hobble, and wild cherry.

Hugh Carter arrived on Thursday leading a spare horse—the reliable Ben. Descent proved somewhat harder than coming up by horseback, since she found herself constantly sliding downward into the saddle horn. She leaned back slightly to make the ride easier for Ben, bracing with the balls of her feet in the stirrups.

She found that she had conquered the sudden dizzying sensation that she had experienced when riding along ledges climbing the mountain. After reaching the stables, Hugh drove her to Myrtle Brown's and, after a brief rest, the old friend took Gracie to the bus station.

Gracie admitted to being so tired that she took a nitro-glycerin tablet, which her doctor had prescribed for feelings of exhaustion. "I was so thankful and happy to have climbed

Mount Le Conte once more, especially after a stroke. During 30 years of nursing, I cared for many sufferers of the condition. Although many were not completely paralyzed, they were never able to overcome its effects enough to resume normal lives," she explained.

With much attention to diet, exercise, and caring for her potted plants, Gracie felt that she gained strength in June, July, and the first part of August. But toward the end of that month she experienced more pains above the waist and general fatigue.

"I tried to rest and take care of myself in September and did not go into the mountains by bus to walk on the trails again, although I walked even more at home. I was very disappointed that my doctor said I couldn't climb Le Conte again by horse to celebrate my 76th birthday as I had celebrated every year since 1954, except one.

"Brooding over the loss of the birthday trip probably led me into making a foolish decision to climb the mountain October 24 without the doctor's knowledge. But in the McNicol family we never said, 'We can't,' but rather, 'We can.' I don't think I can't do something; I just try it and see. It's a lifelong habit.

"Myrtle met me at the bus station in Gatlinburg on October 23 and took me to her house to spend the night so that I could hit the trail after a good night's sleep. She was so wonderful to me that I will never forget those times.

"The weather turned bad and a storm seemed to be brewing, but I had always climbed the mountain on the date set, regardless of weather, including snow and ice, which I usually found on top in April and early November. I gave no thought to turning back.

"Myrtle took me to meet Marvin McCarter of McCarter's Stables in Cherokee Orchard, and I thought I was warmly dressed in thermal underwear and a wool Army shirt bought at the surplus store in Knoxville. But the wind was fierce, with the clouds boiling overhead, and it was bitterly cold, coming right through my heavy clothing.

"Sitting on the horse you get colder than when walking,

because your blood is not circulating as well.... I put my rain-coat on to break the wind and it helped a little. Harry Hanks, the father of a lodge crew member, rode along with us to visit with his son. The horses trotted even more than usual and so I had to rise in the saddle...by the time we reached Rocky Spur—not quite three hours—I was feeling exhausted and had difficulty in breathing as we neared the lodge.

"I didn't say a word to Marvin, but he must have known, because he helped me off the horse and put his arm around me and helped me into the dining hall. When I began to feel even colder inside the lodge, I remembered that was the way the stroke had begun only 10 months before at the church. I drank two cups of very hot coffee, hoping it would improve my circulation, and took a nitroglycerin pill. A doctor who was a guest helped me to my room, and I sank into the big bunk bed and fell asleep immediately.

"I learned later that Marvin had expressed great concern for me, telling some staff members that he feared I would never get off the mountain alive.

"Well, the Good Lord took care of me in spite of my stub-born Scotch ways. That's all that I can say. I felt much bet-ter after a good night's sleep and rested the second day inside the lodge. I went down the third day with Hugh Carter and the packhorses and didn't have any trouble. The weather was much warmer," sighed Gracie, recalling what she said was the only just plain foolish trip she ever made to Le Conte.

Her notebook for 1967 listed only two trips, whereas she had managed five in 1962, the year of the rapids shooting accident. But she wasn't complaining. She had overcome two illnesses which frequently disable people permanently.

"I could not only walk and talk, but I had been able to go home again to Mount Le Conte...it seemed as much a home to me as the trailer. I had not been able to see ahead when I was overworking and eating the wrong things, but God had seen. I vowed to be worthy of His wonderful gift of the out-doors...so perfect, so abundant, so beautiful for everyone to enjoy."

Gracie Three

Bossing one's self is harder than bossing patients in hospitals through the years, Gracie concluded during the "winter bound" months of January and February 1968. She realized that she had a bad habit of thinking about what she would do next while working on something. "It was making me more tired than the work itself...for instance, while cleaning out bureau drawers I'd be thinking about washing down the inside walls of the trailer when it got warmer," she explained.

Since walking cleared her mind of vexations, she would break up the day by strolling to the store in the morning and around the trailer park a couple of times. With the park only a few blocks from downtown Maryville, she could easily walk to the post office, banks, and department stores.

Gracie made no entries in her diary after the stroke in 1967. After her recovery, beginning in the spring of 1968, she carried notepads with her, always recording the number of horseback rides up Le Conte and hikes down. And she listed every wildflower and blossoming tree that she saw throughout the year. Sometimes she commented on other matters.

Determined to pace herself better in 1968 and avoid the near-stroke she feared she had brushed on the second 1967 climb up Mount Le Conte, Gracie attended the wildflower pilgrimage in April and again made two trips up and down the mountain by horse. One was in the spring to catch the height of the wildflower bloom, and the other on October 1 to celebrate her 77th birthday.

Renting horses for the round-trips to the lodge considerably increased costs, because she now had to pay for the bus, the horse, and two nights at the lodge. And she also had medical expenses not encountered before. Wanting to be able to afford to climb the mountain more than twice a year, if physically able, she summoned forth the Scotch management techniques of the McNicols. Meals were planned even more carefully, with not a crumb wasted. All unnecessary lights were turned off, the heat lowered to the minimum, clothes patched, and water use further reduced.

To improve her health, she formed the unvarying habit of resting a few moments when she felt the least bit tired or short of breath throughout 1968 and during the winter of 1969.

When the Smokies loomed on the horizon during clear, blue days of June, she felt in very good shape to make another round-trip by horseback. The lodge register shows this notation beside her usual bold signature: "Up Rainbow by horseback...141 hikes...5 horseback trips...1954 to June 6, 1969...God has been good to me."

Rev. Rufus Morgan noted 96 hikes to the lodge when he signed in during that month. The competition was still on.

Continuing to monitor herself successfully, Gracie made two horseback trips in 1969, one in 1970, and several in 1971.

Always staying at the lodge two nights opened a new pastime for her: discovering wildflower gardens on top or near the top of the mountain.

It was easy to walk to the "saddle" or flat area between the lodge and High Top, or Main Top as old-timers called it, and the grassy turf would be sprinkled with yellow clintonia and wood sorrell in the spring. The bees would cover the mountain honeysuckle blooming there in the summer when angelica would also wave filmy, white clusters in the breeze. Highlights of June in the saddle were the purple blooms of dwarf rhododendron and white flowers on the sand myrtle. Walking in the balsam forest west of the lodge in the area of the first camp near Cliff Top, she would find the sweet white violet in the spring and turtleheads in summer. But Gracie's "garden of gardens" came to be a spot on both sides of the Boulevard Trail, just one-half mile from Myrtle Point. She always tried to go there in July, when these flowers were peaking: Turk's-cap lillies, purple monkshoods, yellow cone flowers, white cohosh, and red bee balm. Most of the plants grew higher than her head, especially monkshood. And the grass of parnassus always awaited her appreciative blue eyes in August and September on the Trillium Gap trail below the spring which supplies the lodge.

During October, wildflowers beckoned from the saddle to Myrtle Point. Every vista featured distant brushes of color on the mountains, foothills, and lowlands. The leaves of the yellow birches would spin like gold coins on the swan-white arms of graceful dancers. Sitting on Cliff Top at midday, she would watch updrafts hurl red and yellow leaves toward her from the tree tops many feet below. It seemed as if the wind had decided to give them a magnificent ride before they reached their destination on the forest floor. Goldenrod and purple and shaggy asters were her favorite wildflowers of October "on top," and she also delighted in the red berries of the mountain ash and witch hobble and the blue berry of the yellow clintonia.

Sometimes guests teased Gracie after hearing her report on what she'd seen in "her garden" that day down on the Boulevard Trail just below Myrtle Point.

"What would Uncle Sam say about your appropriating that for your garden? There are 200 million owners you know!" exclaimed a man from Washington, D.C., one evening.

"I imagine Uncle Sam would say, 'It's their garden, too; why don't they climb Mount Le Conte and see what they have?'" replied Gracie.

One October morning in 1972 she had walked down to the junction of Bullhead and Rainbow Falls trails to see a land- slide, when she noticed a movement below the trail and saw the head of a petite woman coming up. The small woman was alone and carried neither pack nor sweater, although the weather was cool.

The hikers stopped to talk about the wildflowers. The small woman explained that, being unable to get reservations at the lodge, she must hurry back down the mountain in order to reach her Knoxville home by dark.

"Why don't you ask Brownie, the operator of the lodge, if you can bunk with me. There's a two-bunk bed in my room," suggested Gracie. That simple invitation was the beginning of a hiking combination that came to be known at the lodge in a couple of years as "Gracie Three."

On that first day, Anita Crabtree of Knoxville, then age 56, walked to the lodge with Gracie and telephoned her husband, John, a 61-year-old electrical engineer with a utility company, to say that she would not be home for dinner as planned, but would be staying instead at the lodge with a newfound friend from Maryville.

Anita, a former Girl Scout leader, loved the outdoors in general and wildflowers in particular. She was as excited as Gracie, then 81, about finding goldenrod, asters, and gentian blooming beside the Bullhead Trail on their hike down.

Reflecting on that meeting several years later, Anita Crabtree recalled: "I was fascinated with Gracie as soon as we began talking. Her mind is so clear and she is so agile and supple, bending down to pick up a rock and springing up much quicker than I could possibly manage. The more I learned about her, the more I felt that she had grown young hiking the mountain. And she was always doing something to help the staff or other guests at the lodge...it was just her second nature after all those years of nursing, I guessed."

Looking back, Gracie observed that once again people had come into her life when she needed them, although she did not hike again with Anita until the next fall.

The competition between Father Morgan and Gracie for the most trips up the mountain became "hot" in June of 1973. Signing in on May 31, Grace McNicol scrawled beside her name: "141 hikes...15 trips by horse." The total number of trips was, of course, 156. During the next couple of weeks the 86-year-old priest hiked up with a party of friends and former parishioners and listed 136 hikes. Returning for the fifth time that summer on August 20, he wrote firmly: "141 hikes." Someone made a check mark on the register: "A total of 141 hikes up the mountain by each competitor."

By that time Gracie's total included 16 horseback trips in addition to her 141 hikes, and back on June 2 she had ridden a horse up but walked down for the first time since the stroke in 1967. She hiked the seven miles down Bullhead, meeting the taxicab driver as in old times. Her doctor had agreed that she could walk down safely because of her success with regular walks to "garden spots" on top of the mountain and around Maryville. He felt the walk up would still produce too much strain, she said.

Father Morgan was a gentlemanly competitor and usually invited Gracie to join his party at the lodge when they happened to be there at the same time. "I always enjoyed that so much," she recalled.

When the fall artist had once again brushed Le Conte with hues of yellow and red among the greenery and the summit mists were tinged with hints of purple instead of the pinks of summer, Anita Crabtree telephoned from Knoxville to invite Gracie to join the couple for a trip to the lodge. They would pick her up in Maryville and take her to the stables and hike up Alum Cave Bluffs Trail themselves. The three would walk down Bullhead together.

Gracie accepted and telephoned the lodge to see if accommodations were available. They were, and Brownie wrote on the log: Gracie (three).

"So wonderful to walk down Bullhead in October again... Anita and John are perfect company...they're interested in the wildflowers too...and we all keep our eyes open. They don't distract me from enjoying nature.

"We left the lodge in a dripping cloud so heavy we couldn't see out in the open places or very far ahead. The trail was full of leaves, but they were not too slippery. We surprised two grouse on the north slope, and the hen immediately flew away. Not the male. We stood very still. His tail was spread like a fan and his neck feathers were puffed out. He watched

Gracie Three having lunch beside the Alum Cave Bluffs Trail included (from left) Gracie, John Crabtree, and Anita Crabtree. When Gracie kept making reservations for herself and the Crabtrees at the lodge, the crew began writing "Gracie 3" in the book. They gradually began calling the trio of hikers "Gracie Three."

us closely and then strutted away into the woods. Anita and John are very quiet on the trail...they don't scare the birds and animals away like most people do."

They visited Le Conte several times together during 1974, with the reservation always written the same. As the trips continued, the lodge staff began saying "Gracie Three" has this or that cabin, and the nametag stuck...until finally the three hiking companions began referring to themselves in that way.

That is, when they weren't saying something about the "sufferings" of "Poor John." John Crabtree, a trim six-footer, would usually spend the second day hiking down to the trail head where he and Anita had left their car. John would move the car to another trail head and walk back up. That way Anita could enjoying hiking different trails up and down, seeing more wildflowers. If he moved the car from the Alum Cave Bluffs Trail head to Bullhead Trail head, he would have to hike 12 miles for the day. "Well, at least I'm getting enough

Gracie Three with a young couple from Louisiana honeymooning at the lodge in 1977.

exercise," he would say.

It was "Poor John" who took the top bunk when they shared a cabin—usually number five—with Gracie in the bottom bunk and Anita, a demure five-foot-one, sleeping on a cot. An outdoors type who liked to play golf when not hiking, the engineer was a good fire builder, and the women would tease that their fire-building skills were getting rusty because "Poor John" seemed to always reach the cabin first and therefore have to build the fire. The staff usually built fires for guests, but Gracie Three took pride in doing things like that, and the crew probably appreciated the bit of time saved for them.

While the Huffs had tended to hire local people of all ages, the Browns usually worked a college-age crew. Gracie Three enjoyed the young people, finding time to catch up with all the news of what colleges they would be attending during the winter semester and which former staffers had become engaged or married since their last trip.

It was at the end of 1974—Gracie Three's first season of

hiking together—that Herrick and Myrtle Brown ended their 14-year careers as operators of the lodge, although Herrick stayed on in the 1975 season until the new management took over. The Browns' lease with the National Park Service was acquired by three Gatlinburg men: William Rinearson, James H. Ogle, and James A. Huff. Brownie and his wife retired to live in Glendale Springs, North Carolina, on Mount Rogers, two miles off the Blue Ridge Parkway.

It had been 50 years since Paul Adams established the camp that grew into the lodge. It has been estimated that during its first half century almost 400,000 people were overnight guests in the lodge, which has accommodated up to 50 at one time, although the limit in the 1970s was 40 per night.

The news of the Browns' retirement saddened Gracie Three. "When I heard they were leaving, I could have cried," recalled Gracie. "It was just the same as when Pauline Huff left. Myrtle and Brownie had become part of the mountain, and I couldn't imagine the lodge without them. They are such wonderful people, and I will never forget the way they made it possible for me to ascend the mountain again after the stroke by taking me into their home."

Bill Rinearson, one of the three new leaseholders, came up in 1975 to manage the more-than-mile-high hostel. A former ski instructor who loved the outdoors, Bill seemed at home among the frontier-like cabins.

Gracie Three became fond that year of young Debbie Grounds of Michigan, who found her way to Le Conte because she liked to hike and got a job making beds and doing other chores around the lodge. Debbie said that she grew tired of making beds during 1976, her second year on the crew, and decided to try to learn to cook for the guests and staff. Cooking was something of a challenge even for experienced cooks because the 6,593-foot elevation results in a low boiling point.

In the 1970s the lodge served a specific breakfast and dinner menu for its guests because of the problems of transporting food up the mountain and then storing it. There is no electricity. Bottled gas provides for cooking and limited refrigeration.

Horses packed the food and gas up until the mid-1970s, when the practice was begun of bringing in supplies for the entire season by helicopter in the early spring. The National Park Service prohibited transport of food up the mountain trails to the lodge in 1977, with the exception of a small supply of fresh produce for the lodge crew. The move was in response to the protests from environmentalists that the lodge was severely disturbing the ecology of Le Conte. They claimed that the horses' hooves were cutting into the soil and causing erosion. The horses were eventually replaced by llamas because they have padded feet which do not cut into the trail.

After transporting supplies up Mount Le Conte for more than 50 years on packhorses, the lodge began using llamas because their padded feet don't cut into the trails like horses' hooves.

The Park Service also prohibited the lodge from selling drinks or food to hikers who came up on a day hike and did not stay overnight. The food was seen as encouraging more people to climb the mountain, thereby damaging the ecology. Representatives of several conservation groups appeared on the mountain and measured imprints on the trails, counted visitors to the lodge, and observed their activities on top of the mountain. Sitting on the porch of the recreation hall with one of the environmentalists, Bill Rinearson listened to his complaints about the impact of people on the mountain. Rinearson pointed toward Mount Guyot. "Ever been over there?" he asked.

"No, we're just studying this mountain where everybody

comes," was the reply.

"If nobody is impacting Mount Guyot or any of those other mountains—he pointed at all the peaks lining the horizon—is the park really being damaged by our visitors? Folks have been coming up here over 50 years...and the elevation is the same...they haven't worn it down," declared Rinearson.

Both in packhorse and helicopter days the lodge meals for guests remained pretty much the same. Breakfast included pancakes with margarine and syrup, scrambled eggs, scratch biscuits, jelly, coffee, and hot chocolate. Dinner was either canned ham with sweet potatoes and pineapple plus green beans and hot applesauce or canned beef with creamed potatoes, string beans, plus peaches and cookies. A guest staying two nights was not served the same dinner twice.

Crew members spending up to seven months on the mountaintop obviously needed variety in their food. That made the services of a good cook very important. Debbie Grounds, a slender, dark-haired beauty, experimented with herbs to liven up soups and dried bean recipes and concocted a special way of making rolls. She eventually landed the cooking job and also won the heart of Clyde (Rusty) Nail of Knoxville, who signed on in 1976 for general crew work and was soon the person called upon by many to "fix things" around the lodge.

Rusty, a lanky blond frontier type, found many interests in common with Debbie, who was also talented at weaving, sketching, and playing the guitar. They were married at high noon on Cliff Top in the summer of 1977 with Rev. Charles Presley of Cosby officiating. Rusty and Debbie became the managers of the lodge in 1978.

Gracie Three usually tried to bring a fresh treat such as an avocado or a dozen limes or some peaches in their knapsacks to give to the staff for use in preparation of "crew" meals. John sometimes brought ice cream encased in dry ice inside his backpack. That treat was always a big hit.

It was Rusty who suggested that Gracie walk east of the lodge toward the old barn to view the sunset when she didn't feel like hiking to Cliff Top or Myrtle Point. Gracie found the elevated point on the path that afforded a panoramic view over Cliff Top and enjoyed the sun's farewell show on many occasions, standing alone with only the sound of the wind in her ears. She found that on some evenings clouds cover all the mountain ranges to the west so that it looked like an ocean under a deep, blue zenith. The sinking sun would turn the clouds or "ocean" to yellow and pink.

By 1976 Gracie Three had begun coming once per month from April to early November, when the lodge usually closes for the winter. They tried to pick dates when wildflowers would be at peak bloom. At the end of that year Gracie was listing 149 hikes and 46 trips by horseback and Father Morgan 169 hikes. Since Gracie was riding the horse up and hiking down, she began counting two hikes down as one trip and two ascents by horse as one trip.

Some said that Father Morgan definitely considered himself the winner in the competition since Gracie was riding a horse up the mountain. They kidded each other about their tallies.

The Crabtrees were keeping totals by now: 41 for him and 35 for her.

Another change brought about by the complaints of the environmentalists was mandated in the fall of 1976. The superintendent of the Great Smoky Mountains National Park informed the leaseholders that "use of dead and down wood is prohibited to help reduce environmental impacts to an acceptable level." The environmentalists claimed that by burning the downed wood, the lodge was preventing the natural replenishment of the topsoil with decayed wood. The aroma of wood smoke rising from lodge chimneys and cabin flues was replaced with the chemical odor of kerosene. Portable heaters and oil were flown in by helicopter.

Perhaps the lodge lost a touch of frontier hominess, but the major delights of Gracie Three's monthly two-night stays remained the same: walking to Gracie's many "gardens" and enjoying the flowers, trees, and many miles of scenery visible on clear days, plus the fellowship with other hikers and crew members.

About a dozen backpackers were usually staying each night in the Appalachian Trail shelter in the saddle and would join in the fellowship at some point. Gracie pointed out: "All the hikers who come to Le Conte seem alike in their love of nature. They seem to have a peace of soul that comes with the outdoors, and as we rub elbows with each other the love of the mountain becomes stronger. The feeling for nature's peace is even more evident among the lodge staff because they live in the grandeur all season."

Anita's keen interest in wildflowers had begun when she started walking and observing near her Knoxville home in 1966, six years before meeting Gracie. She bought an identification book and began to study, soon becoming a full-fledged wildflower seeker. During her first year of regular hiking, Anita had identified 1,097 different kinds of wildflowers beside the trails. Like Gracie she kept a notebook on hikes at first, but later switched to adding only names of flowers not previously seen to her master list at home. All members of Gracie Three were in agreement that hikers can consistently find more wildflowers blooming along Bullhead than any of the other four main trails on Le Conte.

But Anita's favorite flower garden in the national park in the springtime is Porters Flat, located at the northeastern foot of Le Conte opposite Potato Ridge. It is reached by taking the road through Greenbrier Cove and walking from the old Smoky Mountain Hiking Club cabin.

Anita explained: "The flats are virginal and pure, like a sanctuary. The flowers are growing out of velvet-like green moss that covers logs which lie all over the flats along the creek. Trillium, spring beauty, phacelia, white violets, and rue anemone are so pure and fragile you almost hesitate to speak, fearing the sound of your voice will tarnish them somehow."

Anita's keen interest in keeping records of the wildflowers that she saw encouraged Gracie to make even more complete records of her sightings. Her entries in the notepad carried on one trip up Le Conte provide an example:

"Gracie Three set out for Le Conte when they picked me up at the trailer park at 7:30 a.m. It was an unusually dark and rainy day for May. By 8:30 they left me at the stable and set out to park their car at the trail head and hike up Alum Cave Bluffs Trail. It turned out to be my second fastest trip up the mountain in all these years.

"It was raining hard when I left the stables with Newton Ogle. There were only the two of us and we didn't get on the trail until 12:30 p.m. Newton said he had never been that late and we would have to make up for it. And we sure did. We rode hard, with horses running a lot, in heavy rain, reaching the lodge at 2:30. I can remember going up the mountain in only two hours only one other time—with Tony Ogle. Thankful that my old bones held up...my legs are aching from standing up so much in the stirrups.

"Flowers were beautiful. I saw blooms on white trillium, bluets, white sweet violets, spring beauty, fire cherry, serviceberry, silver bell, mountain fetterbush, sand myrtle, and trailing arbutus.

"The rain has stopped. Spent our second day on the mountain hiking down the Boulevard Trail and sitting around enjoying the views from Myrtle Point and Cliff Top. Anita suggests we 'tally up' our sightings tomorrow on Bullhead.

"Anita and John to bed early while I played Chinese marbles with Mr. White from New York in the recreation room.

"I could tell he was sure that he would beat me. But I held back...the secret in Chinese checkers is patience and waiting...so I waited...and won. Sometimes I wait in vain...but not tonight!

"Third day. 'Poor John' got up early, ate breakfast, and set out to hike the Alum Cave Bluffs Trail down to the highway where the car was parked. He drove it down to the head of Bullhead Trail and then walked up to meet us. Anita and I were sitting in the pine grove counting up our 'sightings' when he arrived. We counted 113 different wildflowers and flowering trees [see page 123 for typical sightings].

"My favorites were corn salad, fire pink, vetch wort, dog

hobble, three-toothed cinquefoil, tulip poplar, sassafras, sweet shrub, princess tree, stone crop, crested iris, many pink lady slippers, bluets, white sweet violets, and trailing arbutus.

"My blessings are so many. God is so good to this wretched sinner who is a sinner by nature saved by the blood of Christ by his salvation, mercy, hope, peace and everlasting love. I thank Him for everything."

Recalling their many "second day" outings on top of Le Conte, Gracie Three seemed fondest of the memories of a brisk October when they decided to spend a whole day on Myrtle Point. They arrived at 9:30 a.m. with lunch plus a thermos of coffee and snacks.

"We found soft spots on rock ledges among the sand myrtle and lay in the sun," Anita remembered. "It was overcast on the north side and sunny on the south, and throughout the day a strong wind blew clouds against the south side of the point, and they would shoot high into the sky. We lay there like lizards, sunning on the rocks, watching the clouds...you could almost let your mind fly free with those clouds as they rose into the heavens. I don't think I've ever been more relaxed in my life. We didn't return to the lodge until four o'clock. No one needed a nap before dinner that day."

Gracie said that Anita soon became known as the "sunrise woman" as Gracie Three stayed regularly at the lodge. Learning the times of sunrises from the lodge's list in the dining room, she would set her pocket alarm clock in order to rise and hike in darkness the mile to Myrtle Point in time to view the sunrise. She always carried a flashlight but didn't always use it. "I knew that path from memory, and it was lined much of the way by high laurel bushes. You couldn't stray off...I never met a bear in the dark...but usually carried a stick, just in case," said Anita. Guests inquiring about the sunrise were usually referred by the staff to Anita, who made a note to knock on their doors in the early morning before she departed, many times alone, for the point.

John preferred to remain in bed, and Gracie, who in her

Gracie (just to the left of the camera) and hikers from several states sit on Cliff Top awaiting one of Mount Le Conte's storied sunsets. Gracie enjoyed joining hands with other hikers here and singing as the sun disappeared over the horizon. Favorite songs were "Amazing Grace" and "Go Tell It on the Mountain."

early years on the mountain saw most sunrises at Myrtle Point, after her stroke chose instead to view the sunrise halfway to High Top, thereby conserving her strength for "second day" treks to wildflower gardens.

But Gracie considered Myrtle Point the best sunrise overlook. Sometimes the skies would be overcast and the hiker knew the day had come only because the darkness had thinned. At such times the point was so shrouded in thick fog and clouds that hikers couldn't see a laurel bush twenty feet away. It was a moody and mysterious experience.

A spectacle of magnificent splendor awaits on those mornings when the tops of mountains, ridges, and foothills rise dusky green from valley and ravines filled with drifting mist. The green crests of land float in seas of clouds as far as the eye can see. A sudden quickening seems to fill the air and still the viewer's breath as tints of orange, gold, yellow, and soft reds appear in the east, growing ever larger and larger until the full light of the ball of fire forces the eyes down to the clouds below.

As nature's chariot of energy streaks upward, the clouds are tinged momentarily with gold and seem to begin disappearing under the green mountaintop vessels sailing serenely only moments before. The new fiery presence dominating the world of Mount Le Conte soon burns the clouds away to reveal the Great Smokies in undulating ripples of all the shades of green that one could ever imagine. The word "aurora" must have been created on Myrtle Point, a hiker once said.

Hikers usually encounter snow and ice on climbs made in March and late October, and after weather fronts have moved through, the lower mountaintops turn into hundreds of jeweled crowns reflecting aurora's fire in the Myrtle Point panorama.

Gracie recalled an experience in late October on Le Conte in which the entire top of the mountain turned into a crown of crystal. Gracie Three had left Maryville with the temperature about 72 degrees. The themometer fell sharply as they and other lodge guests watched the sunset from Cliff Top. A scientist from Oak Ridge had a big laboratory themometer on which they watched the mercury drop. It stopped at 28 degrees.

"During the night I awoke cold in spite of my thermal underwear and the Hudson Bay blankets...I called to Anita, and she was freezing too. 'Poor John' climbed out of the top bunk and started a big fire in the heater. He checked his thermometer and it was 17 degrees. He stayed up a couple of hours keeping the fire going, and then I got up and relieved him.

"Anita decided it was too cold to go see the sunrise...so she shut off the alarm. We got out of bed when the sun shone in the window. We could not believe our eyes. Everything was covered with shards of ice, glistening in the sun. The shards were about an inch long. Anita and John said it was a hoar frost. The fog had frozen on everything when the temperature fell so sharply.

"We dressed quickly and went outside. All the guests were out taking pictures. Brownie came out and told us breakfast would be an hour late to give everyone time to enjoy the hoar frost. We were dazzled by the shimmering shards of ice. They covered the roofs of the buildings, every twig on the trees, every weed, every rock, every seed, everything.

"Most of us went to Cliff Top, where the laurel and sand myrtle were competely outlined in the ice shards. The sky was blue without a single cloud overhead. All around the horizon was a ring of low white clouds...the ring was completely even, as if designed that way. We used up all of our film, and most other folks did too, and finally went to breakfast.

"We spent about 45 minutes eating pancakes and all the trimmings and drinking coffee and talking about the hoar frost. When we came outside the sun had melted everything that was not in shade. The frost was gone.

"We found about 50 dead birds in and around the woodshed. They were small yellow birds, and no one seemed to know what kind of bird. We assumed that they had been migrating south in the warm weather and had been caught unexpectedly by the sudden drop in temperature. The Oak Ridge scientist volunteered to take a few dead bird specimen to the naturalist at National Park Service headquarters near Gatlinburg. I've seen several other hoar frosts, but nothing as magnificent as that one."

Recalling all the good times experienced by Gracie Three, Gracie said that it just proved once again that sometimes folks would come into your life when you needed them most. "I only hope that I have meant something to people the way Carl, Eula, John, and Anita, and some other friends have affected me," said Gracie softly.

Gracie reaches the Alum Cave Bluffs Trail head on U.S. Highway 441 after marking her 200th trip up Le Conte. She holds the "champion hiker" trophy awarded to her in ceremonies on top the night before.

Gracie signs autographs for friends in the recreation hall at the lodge.

Trip 200: A Milestone, Not a Destination

Gracie was even more restless than usual with her winter months' routine during January and February of 1977. Walks around the trailer park and downtown Maryville didn't seem to help much. Her thoughts were on Mount Le Conte most of the time, and the date March 29 kept popping up often because reaching a special goal she had set was almost within grasp: making her 200th trip up the mountain.

Gracie Three had reservations at the lodge for March 29 and once every month thereafter, to end with a stay planned for November 1-3. The trip set for March 29 would be her 196th, and she could mark 200 in July "if God would permit."

Was she eager to reach that goal because no other climbers—other than lodge personnel—were known to have attained it, or because she just wanted to prove to herself that she could? "Prove it to myself," she answered with a big McNicol grin. She would be 86 years old on October 1, and her doctor had given full approval to her habit of riding up, spending two nights, walking atop the mountain, and walking down since 1972.

"I seemed to have disciplined myself pretty well after the foolish trip [October of 1967] nine months after my stroke. So I continued to try to concentrate on doing what I wanted to do, but at the same time going slowly enough not to be in trouble before I discovered I was trying too much," Gracie explained.

As she made preparations for the beginning of what she

hoped would be a record-setting hiking season, Gracie's days were highlighted with her notes on the positions of the sun, moon, and stars in relation to the tops of the old maples which give Shady Grove Trailer Park its name. Some people might think it implausible for a nature-lover to live in the midst of about 30 mobile homes set fairly close together, but others tend to believe you can find whatever you are seeking anywhere, if you try.

She kept up with the stages of the moon and expected risings and settings of the sun and moon in the newspapers and by radio. Although television had become increasingly popular with Americans since her first Le Conte climb 23 years before, Gracie still had no desire or time for a set. She was too busy learning more about the natural world, having only to look out the window to become fascinated by a bird sitting on the fence surrounding her 21-by-40-foot yard.

Snow and ice were reported at the higher elevations on Le Conte when March 29 arrived, but Gracie had always told Marvin McCarter: "If the horse can go, I can go."

The lodge had been open to guests about five days. Like any good hiker, Gracie always dressed in layers so that she could remove and replace clothing according to temperature changes. For this trip up by horse, she was wearing the usual cold weather garb: a billed cap from river rapid days (the bill kept rain off her glasses), thermal underwear, pajamas, jeans, flannel shirt, a heavy wool jacket-shirt, a lap robe, and raincoat.

The possibility of finding unusual weather on Le Conte added to the excitement as she and longtime friend Newton Ogle of McCarter's headed up the trail, with Gracie riding a horse named Sugar Boy. Gracie always enjoyed Newton because she said he knew the names of all the trees and wildflowers. "I depend on him to keep me straight," she'd say.

The riders saw yellow and purple violets blooming along the bridle trail in the 2,600- to 4,000-feet-above-sea-level area below Rainbow Falls. As they rested at the falls, she made a note that some ice needles hung from rocks and the air was cold.

The wind was sharp on Rocky Spur and the sky overcast. They pushed ahead to the junction of Rainbow Falls and Bullhead trails "and went from spring into winter," Gracie said.

"The ground was covered with snow and ice and the wind blew fiercely. The horses' feet began to slip, and I gave Sugar Boy full reign so that he could look closely at the trail and pick his way along. Newton's horse was slipping very badly, and they later joked it was because he wouldn't put his head down as far as Sugar Boy to see the trail."

The lodge's cabins and shingled dining hall were covered with snow, and the scene could easily have been an artist's painting of an outpost in early American days. Anita and John had already arrived, having come up Alum Cave Trail where they encountered deep snow and ice near the top. Like Gracie, they dressed for all kinds of weather for hikes in early spring and late fall, so they had emerged in good shape.

The hikers, who had come up from all directions, sat around the kerosene heater in the recreation hall (built during the Browns' tenure) and exchanged stories of the hardships of their climbs.

"The heat felt so good in the bitter cold that we forgot to be sorry we were not sitting around a fireplace filled with blazing balsam logs as in former times," recalled Gracie.

As is the way in the springtime, the weather moderated during the

A *National Geographic* photographer made this picture of Gracie when they happened to be at the lodge at the same time in 1977.

night and rain melted most of the snow and ice. Gracie's notes show that more than two inches fell the next day, and Gracie Three relaxed in their cabin and caught up on the winter news of the members of the lodge staff.

David Witherspoon of Florida, a staff member for several years who had spent the winter of 1976-77 in the lodge just as he had done for the two before that, told about the many days and nights when the mercury fell below zero and of using snowshoes to move about on the mountaintop. Until the early 1970s the lodge had just been locked up during the off-season—its wooden shutters clamped down. But due to the increased number of hikers in the Smokies, leaseholders found it necessary to have someone stay while the lodge was closed for four months.

Being up-to-date on Le Conte news and well-rested after a day in their cabin, Gracie Three was in fine shape to hike to Myrtle Point after dinner. The downpour of rain had stopped in late afternoon, and the day ended peacefully with the trio watching a bright yellow moon sailing over a sea of clouds.

Their efforts in making a March climb were well rewarded with sightings of 26 blooming wildflowers and trees, including redbud, serviceberry, and dogwood, as they walked down Bullhead on March 31. The day was sunny and clear, and snow and ice seemed ages past.

The pages of Gracie's 1977 notebook are filled with her jottings on nature's wonders as she made trips 197, 198, and 199. Trip number 200 was scheduled for July 12-14, with the 13th being the 52nd anniversary of the day in 1925 when Paul Adams, three teenage boys, and a German shepherd dog climbed Le Conte via Rainbow Falls to establish their camp.

On July 12 Newton Ogle was the guide from McCarter's stables, and he led the way for Gracie and six other riders up Trillium Gap Trail. At lower elevations it was sunny with broken clouds, and the top of Le Conte was overcast. Groves of rhododendron were filled with snow-white blooms, and orange Turk's-cap lillies and red bee balm waved bright greetings as the horses passed. They saw two rare purple fringed orchids. When the party arrived at the lodge, John and Anita were unpacking their gear and talking about the flowers that they had seen in "Gracie's garden" on their trip up the Boulevard Trail.

Grace McNicol signed the register: 149 hikes and 51 trips up by horse...200 trips. At that time her closest competitor, Father Morgan, listed 170 hikes. John Crabtree, having been able to hike more since retiring, had signed in with 51 trips, and Anita had a total of 41.

Gracie Three walked down Boulevard Trail about two miles to meet Robert Dougherty of Knoxville, Gracie's 44-year-old nephew, who was coming up to celebrate her record. The group rested at "Gracie's garden" and counted the number of flowers blooming.

The lodge crew staged a 200-trip party at five o'clock before the regular 6:00 p.m. dinner. The Crabtrees presented an engraved trophy to Gracie as "champion hiker," and the lodge crew's commemorations were a leather plaque made by

Celebrating her 200th trip up Mount Le Conte, Gracie shows a young couple the engraved leather plaque that lodge crew members made for her.

Wally Evans and an aluminum plate engraved with the names of each member of the crew and stating the purpose of the award. The plate was from the metal camp-type service used at the lodge for many years before the 1970s. The crew included Rusty and Debbie Nail, Wally Evans, Tim Line, Debbie Scott, and Enid Schenk.

"Oh, they spoil me so up there," laughed Gracie, her blue eyes aglow as she waved at the mementos displayed in her trailer. A brilliant sunset at Cliff Top was a fitting end for her 200-trip day, Gracie said.

The trip was a milestone—not a destination. Gracie was destined to make 44 more trips up the mountain. Gracie Three returned five times in 1977, celebrating Gracie's 86th birthday with a candle in a blueberry pancake at breakfast on October 1, 1977. A special surprise was having two old friends arrive to celebrate with her: Eula Fry and Millie Shields. They relived the "500-mile" year and many other feats of a decade before, talking for hours.

Notepads that Gracie carried on her trips to jot down wildflowers on the spot show a variety of activities for the next six years. Some representative entries are listed below.

"May 4, 1980. Gracie Three drove to Chilhowee Mountain, looking for pink lady slippers. We found many—some in full bloom and others not out good. Don't find lady slippers very often."

"Enjoyed singing in the recreation hall with an interdenominational church youth group from Ohio. The church groups are always singing. Had a lot of fun two trips ago singing with a group of 14 Catholic friends from Knoxville. They included Sisters Mary Janice and Marie Moore. Most of the group belonged to a choir at their church."

"I was undressing in Cabin Five when a bear pushed the door open and started in. Tim Line ran toward her with a broom and she dashed away. Then he shot at her with his harmless air rifle. The bear's hair was so thick, the pellets probably didn't go through. I thanked Tim for watching out for me."

"Did not have regular trip up Le Conte scheduled, but

Gracie finds a spot on Cliff Top to await the sunset. Although most visitors view the sunset at Cliff Top, Gracie also enjoyed watching it at High Top and Myrtle Point.

since John was going over the mountain, he took me to Alum Cave Bluffs Trail Head and I hiked up to Gracie's Pulpit. I ate my lunch in that sacred spot and then sat looking at Le Conte and meditating on God's holy word. I was alone but not alone because God was there. I rejoiced in the beauty of the trees and flowers and praised His holy name.

"I hiked back down and caught the bus out on Highway 441 and made the trip through Gatlinburg and Knoxville as usual."

Gracie was eager to climb the mountain to celebrate her 90th birthday on October 1, 1981. Just to be on the safe side, she decided to ride both up and down. It proved an exciting trip. She filled six pages in her notepad:

"Enjoyed eating blackberries and blueberries on our way up the Rainbow Falls Trail. Everyone soon had 'black' teeth. Saw asters, red berries on the mountain ash and on the red-berried elder and blue berries on the yellow clintonia.

"Spent entire day on top at Myrtle Point with two women Presbyterian ministers, Carol Brown of Manchester, Kentucky, and Paige Brady. We talked about the majesty of God reflected everywhere in the view from Myrtle Point. When we ate our sandwiches for lunch, they said beautiful prayers.

"The dinner bell rang and when we got to the dining hall, everything was covered with streamers made of sheets held in place with festoons of red mountain ash berries. They all started singing 'happy birthday' to me and brought out a fancy cake baked by Lisa Line. It was 2-tiered held up by glasses and also decorated with red mountain ash berries. Balloons were everywhere. I like excitement and there was excitement to spare. The woman minister from Kentucky prayed a most thoughtful blessing. You would have thought that she had known me for years and we met for the first time that day on Myrtle Point. They gave me all sorts of warm socks, sweaters and things. But most wonderful of all, Anita passed around a notebook and asked everyone to write a birthday note to me.

"Going down the mountain on Rainbow Falls Trail brought some surprises. Lessie McCarter of McCarter's Stables was the guide. Two couples were riding down with us along with two spare horses. One woman riding behind me fell off of her horse, rolling in front of the horse's front feet. Lessie helped her back on the horse and told her how to hold the reins and keep her feet in the stirrups.

"The woman kept fidgeting and squirming and fell off two more times. Lessie was puzzled as to what to do. She gave the reins on her horse to the man handling the spare horses to take over that horse too. Then she started walking in the rocky trail, leading the horse of the woman who kept falling. She told her to hold tight onto the saddle horn. It was slow going.

"When we got to Rainbow Falls Lessie asked me to ride ahead and tell Marvin McCarter to send help up to her. I hit my horse Ribbon hard on the rump to get her away from the other horses. So away we went for two and one-half miles. I kept the balls of my feet hard in the stirrups, and thought 'what a fine way to start my 91st year—riding high and free

Gracie and Marvin McCarter of McCarter's Stables head up Mount Le Conte. Gracie is riding Sugar Boy, one of her favorite horses, on one of the 89 horseback trips she made up the mountain. At age 90 she raced a horse two and one-half miles from Rainbow Falls to Chero-kee Orchard to seek help for the horse crew following her on the trail.

on the mountain.'

"I was alone and so happy, riding fast on a good horse. And I was able to help someone else. Ribbon seemed happy to be racing down the mountain too.

"I reached the parking lot about 5:00 o'clock. John and Anita were waiting for me and Marvin rode up in his truck.

"When I told him what had happened, he said, 'If a 90-year-old woman can ride a horse down the mountain that woman should at least be able to sit on one without falling off...but then you've been riding with us 17 years.'

"Marvin got on Ribbon and rode away up the mountain to help Lessie. Thank you God once again for helping me through danger. Thank you for holding my old bones together on that flying horse."

Gracie greatly enjoyed reading her birthday notebook. Some of the notes had been collected in advance from people who were unable to come up for the party.

Anita Crabtree wrote: "On your 90th birthday, I want to thank you for the nine memorable years you have had me under your wing. May the next nine be as memorable and rewarding for you and for me. May God bless and keep you now and always."

Mrs. Edward Phifer, Jr., of Morganton, North Carolina, wrote: "I admire you. I'm almost 69 and have only been up here about six times. So I'll never catch up with you, but I'll keep coming as long as I am able."

The note from Rob Ingram of Greeneville, Tennesseee: "I enjoyed meeting you. Your accomplishments of hiking these mountains will always inspire me as I walk. I only hope I can walk as long as you have."

Both Tim and Lisa Line, who had been managers of the lodge for several years, wrote notes. Lisa said: "We are so happy to be celebrating this day with you. You are a special ornament to the mountains—as lovely as any bird or flower—and I am thankful for you as I am for them. May you go on gracing the mountains for a long time. We love you. May your loving God always keep you."

Tim wrote: "Gracie, we're all very fortunate to have you

spend your birthday up here on 'your' mountain. I look forward to your trips and will continue to do so for the next 50 years."

Herrick Brown added this note: "I well remember our first meeting—out in the woodyard in 1960. Joe Trentham was here and introduced you. Never thought I'd see this 21 years later. Congratulations! Keep it up."

Myrtle Brown was succinct: "You are an inspiration to us all."

Dr. and Mrs. A. M. Lang of North Carolina wrote: "Thanks for letting us enjoy your birthday party. We had read of you but had no idea we would be so lucky as to meet you. God bless you."

When Gracie talked about the people who had come into her life and helped her so much, she always mentioned Emily Wessel of Newburgh, Indiana. After meeting at the wildflower pilgrimage in Gatlinburg, Gracie and Emily hiked several trails on the pilgrimage together. Emily was to return almost every year for the remainder of Gracie's life. They went up Mount Le Conte many times. Emily met the Reverend Morgan on the mountain and on two occasions took Gracie to Franklin, North Carolina, to attend one of his services in the little chapel with the window behind the altar.

Before climbing Le Conte together on September 30, 1982, Emily arrived early and invited Gracie to travel with her and her four Russian wolfhounds (borzoi), which she raised, by station wagon to Franklin, North Carolina, to visit Father Morgan. They spent one night in the cabin where the priest was born. His daughter Frances was living there at the time.

Gracie recorded the visit in her notepad: "Traveled to Franklin September 26 with Emily and four dogs to visit Rufus Morgan, who will be 97 years old October 15. He looked just fine and we joked about both being born under the zodiac sign of Libra. We agreed that we do want everything in balance and under control.

"I told him I was going to match his record of climbing Le Conte at age 92 next year. He said that I am never going to match his hiking record, if I don't stop riding a horse up. I told him he ought to try riding a horse...that he would find it wasn't so easy!

"We talked about our many trips up Le Conte, and he asked me to tell him about all the glorious wildflowers I had seen lately. I assured him that the grass of parnassus simply covered the area around the spring in August and early September. I described the shabby asters, angelica, turtlehead, monkshood, and bee balm that I had seen.

"I also mentioned how sad it was to see some of the balsam fir trees around the lodge dying, apparently because of an infestation of wooly moth. He said, 'Oh, the wonderful fir trees on Le Conte...the eternal green mantle. They remind me of what Hosea says in the Bible, 'I am like a green fir tree. From me is thy fruit found.'

"He said that Hosea was comparing the redeemed Israel to the fruitful, evergreen fir tree. Then he talked a lot about all the plants mentioned in the Bible, even mustard. And he recited a verse from Luke: 'It is like a grain of mustard seed, which a man took, and cast into his garden; and it grew, and waxed a great tree.'

"Father Morgan said that was a parable used by Jesus to compare the fast growth of the gospel message to the rapid development of the tiny mustard seed into a giant plant. He is so amazing. Ever since I first met him, he has quoted scripture word for word. I think he must have memorized the whole Bible."

Returning to Tennessee, Emily Wessel accompanied Gracie up the mountain to celebrate her 91st birthday on October 1. They rode up Rainbow Falls trail. It was Gracie's 236th trip—155 hikes and 81 horse climbs. Ginger Kelly of Gatlinburg, mother-in-law of Peter McCarter, rode up with them. Newton Ogle was the guide.

"I am going to be a grandmother! Lisa and Tim told us they will have a baby in March. They are going to move the supplies out of the dining hall building and store them in the end of the recreation building. That way they can live in the storage room and Lisa can look after the baby while cooking and meeting guests in the kitchen and dining rooms. It will be hard work, but I believe that Lisa can manage anything. She is so thoughtful and talented...such a fine young couple. They will make good parents."

Gracie climbed the mountain again on October 27, 1982. An old friend, Barbara Renfro of Knoxville, had driven Gracie to the Rainbow Falls Trail head in Cherokee Orchard, and she rode up with Newton Ogle. They got a late start because Newton had to shoe a couple of horses on the spot.

That night Gracie wrote, "I hadn't seen anyone shoe a horse since I was back on the farm in Kansas. I had great luck. Brownie [Herrick Brown] dropped by to say hello. We all ate with the crew—chicken pie and baked apples. Later that evening we stood outside enjoying the full moon and a sky covered with stars. I thank God for all his creations."

She wrote two pages on her second night at the lodge: "Met someone tonight who has made many more trips to Le Conte than I: John Longstreet, the pilot of the helicopter which brings supplies and sometimes carries injured persons away to a hospital. Today he came up for the 361st time. I ate supper with him and Don Rivard, the co-pilot, and Donnie Zueber, the mechanic. John flew on the pipe lines in Alaska for awhile. We had a wonderful time telling tales about Alaska. We both admitted that we miss it sometimes. I know I won't be going back, and he doesn't think he will either."

She rode down Trillium Gap Trail with Newton Ogle. They met Robert Dougherty about halfway down. A skilled photographer, he came to meet Gracie and photograph the fall colors. "The yellow and red maples were simply glowing against backgrounds of green hemlock," noted Gracie.

Gracie missed her sister Ruth in the winter of 1981-82 because she had moved to Kansas to live after her husband died. But she visited often with the Robert Dougherty family, who lived between Clinton and Knoxville. And old friends like Barbara Renfro continued to drop by.

Bill Rinearson came by her home several times that winter and took her on automobile rides in the Smokies. They drove around Cades Cove some. "Counted 104 deer and saw several turkeys, skunks, and one ground hog," noted Gracie after one ride in the cove.

Gracie began 1983 with a grand flight to Green Valley, Arizona, to help her brother Ralph celebrate his 100th birthday on March 5. Ruth and her son, Robert, went also. Ralph's children and grandchildren and many other friends and family joined in. For the occasion Gracie wore the wool suit she'd had constructed from the official McNicol plaid, which she had ordered from somewhere in Scotland. Gracie set another goal for herself: "Living to reach 100 just like Ralph." He lived four more years.

During the 1983 season, Gracie Three went up Mount Le Conte every month from April through October, when she reached the goal of celebrating her 92nd birthday.

The August trip was the last recorded in Gracie's notepad. She apparently made no notes on her birthday trip of September 30-October 2. Following is the last trip recorded in Gracie's notepad:

"August 22, 1983. Trip 243—155 hikes and 88 by horse. Newton Ogle was the guide up Rainbow Falls Trail. Four other riders were with us. It was very hazy. Saw green cone flower, shabby asters, snakeroot, daisies, red bee-balm, monkshood, berries on witch hobble. Went through rain with some lightning. We arrived at the lodge at noon. I took a nap and visited with other guests before dinner. I went to High Top to see the sunset. Tim said it reached 76 degrees today. Highest was 80 degrees years ago.

"August 23. Slept good between sheets and all blankets last night. Day was clear and sunshiny. Walked down Trillium Gap Trail...still few grass of parnassus blooming. Saw shabby asters, ferns, moss. Ate my sandwich for lunch beside Trillium.

"Back at the lodge, they asked me to move from Cabin 3 to my old room behind the fireplace in the old lodge. That's a favorite place and I was glad to move. Enjoyed visiting with Ken Wright, a hiker I've known for years. He comes up and stays from three days to a week at a time. We talked about the time we were together here in a storm. We watched the wind blow trees down, but felt secure in our log cabin.

"Later I walked around in the trees beside the lodge, talking with a surgical nurse, who had come up for the night. From what she said, things are changing a lot in hospitals. Guess I would be completely lost now in all the high technology. At least I don't have to worry about working third shift anymore. She said she rotates around three shifts, working two weeks each one. She has a family so it must be very difficult for her.

"August 24, 1983. Newton Ogle arrived at noon. He brought a good horse named Sandy for me to ride down. We left at 12:15 p.m., going down Trillium Gap Trail. When we got among the trees where the trail is wide and smooth our horses began to trot. I braced myself in the saddle and, fortunately held to the saddle horn with one hand. Suddenly Sandy started bucking and I felt myself going up in the air. Newton yelled 'keep her going.'

"I managed to hang on and gradually stopped the horse. Newton looked at Sandy and found where hornets had stung him on the belly. He got a spray can of insecticide out of his pack, and went back up the trail and found the nest near the bottom of a tree. He sprayed them good.

"I petted Sandy on the neck and he calmed down. The rest of the way seemed easy after that. I saw lots of red bee balm and some turk's-cap lillies.

"After almost 19 years of riding the horses up and down the mountains that was my first time to be on a bucking horse. It was the first time in my 92 years really...I was afraid old Nell would buck at home, but she never did that I remember.

"God has sheltered me from harm again. May I be sanctified wholly to God. Help me to do His work, walk always in His way, and follow Him always, doing His will."

Gracie signed in at the lodge on her 244th trip on September 30, 1983. It marked 155 hikes and 89 by horseback. Although no notes of that trip remain, one can imagine that the 92nd birthday celebration was in the style to which she had become accustomed over the years, with much fanfare and loving tribute. Gracie had achieved her longtime goal:

matching Father Morgan's feat of climbing the mountain at the age of 92.

The following spring Gracie's doctor said that she could not go up the mountain by horse because she was having trouble maintaining her balance. She was plagued with incidents of vertigo. Within a few months she sold her trailer and moved into Candleridge Plaza Apartments in Powell, Tennessee, between Knoxville and Clinton. Ruth had returned to the area and also rented an apartment at Candleridge Plaza.

The two greatly enjoyed visiting back and forth and going out to breakfast often with Ruth's son, Robert Dougherty. He took them to their favorite breakfast buffet spot, Shoney's.

Having more room in the apartment than in the trailer, Gracie had pictures and mementos of her Le Conte trips displayed all around. While living at Candleridge, she had a distinguished visitor, a newsman from the staff of Charles Kuralt, the nationally famous radio and television newsman. Kuralt had heard about this woman in her nineties being the most frequent visitor to the Le Conte lodge.

The newsman asked Gracie to tell how she felt about Le Conte and her many trips. The interview was broadcast nationwide on Kuralt's radio program *Exploring America*. The interview included her descripton of how it felt to be a "90-year-old girl on high" riding a horse fast down the mountain.

Kuralt called her "One tireless American, tireless in the pursuit of her dreams...an original spirit in a land of originals."

Many friends from her Le Conte days came to call. Lisa and Tim Line dropped by to introduce her to her namesake: their new baby daughter, Gracie. Their son, Nathan, was a bouncing two-year-old. Gracie was proud of her "grandchildren" and always kept their pictures up for all to see.

Several years later Emily Wessel would give little Grace a historic quilt. Earlier Gracie had given the quilt that she had pieced at age 11 to Emily. "I felt her namesake should have it," said Emily. "We old-timers from Le Conte days are family."

Lisa and Tim Line, managers of Mount Le Conte Lodge for a number of years, hold their children Nathan (right) and Gracie. Their daughter is the namesake of their frequent guest Grace McNicol, who was delighted with her "grandchildren."

In her 96th year, Gracie was still one to spring up and down as always. One day she was perching atop a kitchen stool when she bent sideways to pick up something on the counter. The uneven weight in the awkward position broke her hip. A couple of weeks in the hospital and two or three months in the Knoxville Convalescent Center followed. She could not continue to live independently.

Gracie moved to the Anderson County Nursing Home in Clinton. The imbalance persisted, but she resisted using a cane to walk down the corridors in the nursing home. She would walk close to the wall and steady herself with her hands if she felt dizzy. "I've always been able to walk out of my troubles. I'll do it again," she would say to Anita and other friends and family.

When Gracie was about 98 years old, Emily Wessel surprised her with an invitation for a drive in her van. "I stopped by on my way to Gatlinburg to the annual wildflower pilgrimage. I took Gracie to a place where I'd found some pink lady slippers blooming beside the road. Her vision was failing and she had to get down on her knees to see them. But she was so thrilled when she picked them out."

This author visited Gracie at the Oak Ridge Hospital in the summer of 1991. She was having more problems with her hip. Although barely able to see me, she began an animated conversation upon realizing who I was. "I'm climbing Mount Le Conte in my mind this year," she said, "I can almost see the red bee balm and turtleheads blooming beside the Bullhead Trail."

Grace Viola McNicol died as the result of pneumonia on September 10, 1991, only 20 days before her 100th birthday. Robert Dougherty said that, unknown to Gracie, family and friends were trying to arrange a helicopter trip to Le Conte to celebrate the goal of 100 years that Gracie had vowed to reach. They had been concerned that her health would not permit the flight.

"One of the last times we saw her, my wife, Barbara, asked Gracie what she wanted for her birthday. Gracie answered immediately: '100 cones of my favorite ice cream,'" recalled Robert. "She was a positive, upbeat person to the very last."

Her body was buried in the Lynch-Bethel Cemetery in the Karns Community between Knoxville and Clinton.

Sir Edmund Percival Hillary, one of the first two men to reach the top of Mount Everest, once gave this explanation for their conquest: "We climbed because nobody climbed it before—it was a mountain to climb."

But that did not seem to be Grace McNicol's reason. In an explanation alluded to in the interview on the Kuralt program, Gracie said "I feel closest to God on Mount Le Conte when I am among all the splendor He has created for us to enjoy...from the tiniest spring beauty flower to the mountain itself and the stars in the heavens above. The Bible says, 'He causeth His wind to blow, and the waters flow.'

"Sometimes when I sit on Myrtle Point and see the mountain spread out before me, I feel that my spirit sweeps up like an eagle, flying over the tops of the far ranges, swooping down to drink in the sparkling waters of the streams and sailing over Anakeesta Ridge to get a closer look at a Turk's-cap lily blooming beside the Boulevard Trail."

Gracie's Le Conte Wildflower Notebook
Compiled in 1977, Her 200th-Trip Year

(Note: Usually only blooming flowers and trees are listed. Plants are not written in the order they were seen beside the trails and on top of the mountain, because random jottings were put together at the lodge and at home.)

MARCH — 29th, up Rainbow Falls Trail, snow and ice last half-mile; violets (yellow, purple, white sweet), bloodroot (white bloom), anemone, hepatica, many trailing arbutus (white and pink). 30th, on top, no flowers seen because of more than two inches of rainfall which stopped before night, bright moon, only traces of snow remain. 31st, down by Bullhead Trail, few traces of snow, sunny and clear; anemone (rue and wood), violets (purple, yellow, round, birdfoot, downy and Halberd leaved), cinquefoil, dutchman's-breeches, yellowroot shrub, squirrel corn, trailing arbutus (many), hepatica, early meadow rue, bloodroot, periwinkle, serviceberry, redbud, dogwood, red maple, trout lily, bishop's cap, grandiflorum trillium (pure white with yellow center), silverbell, pussy toes, magnolia (in bud), spring beauty (most of these are about two weeks early).

APRIL — 12th, up Rainbow Falls Trail, sunny and clear; apple blossoms (Cherokee Orchard), violets (purple, yellow, white sweet), trillium (erect, grandiflorum, painted), chickweed, anemone, trout lily, trailing arbutus, bishop's cap, bluets, devil's-bit, dogwood, foamflower. Many stars visible at night on top; 13th, clear and pretty on top. 14th, saw sunrise at Myrtle Point, day clear and sunny; down Bullhead Trail; dogwood, serviceberry, buckeye, cherry, magnolia, apple, silverbell, yellow violets (also round, Halberd leaved and downy), Canada violet, sweet white and purple violets, painted trillium, spring beauty, bishop's cap, dutchman's-breeches, squirrel corn, showy orchis, birdfoot violet, trout lily, wild oats, oval rag wort, louse wort, fire pink, Solomon's-seal (both true and false), yellow root, smooth rock cress, chickweed, merrybell, columbine, anemone (true and wood), crested iris, tulip tree, stonecrop, trailing arbutus, blue cohosh, early meadow rue, pussy toes, pink lady's slippers (once counted over 200 in this spot of pine trees, less than half that today), bluets, periwinkle, fleabane, strawberry.

MAY — 17th, up by Trillium Gap Trail, weather warm, humid and hazy; dog-hobble, bluets, Canada and sweet white violets, red trillium, erect trillium, red-berried elder blooms, galax, foamflower, chickweed, umbrella-leaf, cherry, wood-sorrel, silverbell, yellow clintonia, buckeye, witch-hobble (hobblebush), Fraser's sedge; on top napped on rock in sun in late afternoon on Myrtle Point, many stars at night. 18th, from Myrtle Point see Venus in east then mountain ranges come in view one after another in dark blue as sun rises; walked down Boulevard Trail with Anita Crabtree finding 179 painted trillium, many erect trillium, blood trout lily; rain poured on way back to lodge; 19th, down Bullhead Trail, weather sunny, violets (Canada, sweet white, northern white, and one unknown), erect trillium, white and pink trilliums, Indian-pipe, cherry, many mountain laurel, buckeye, silverbell, Fraser magnolia, umbrella-leaf, yarrow, toothwort, Solomon's seal (true and false), spring beauty, bluets, sand myrtle, purple rhododendron (early), skunk currants, mountain cress, flame azalea, stonecrop, dutchman's-pipe, gooseberry, blackberry, sweet cicely, clintonia (both white and yellow), trout lily, purple bluets, rosy twisted-stalk, saxifrage, dewberry, pussy toes, red clover, butterfly weed,

Queen Anne's lace, white clover, crown clover, striped maple, white fringed phacelia, hearts-a-bustin' (blooms), ox-eye daisy, woodland chickweed, painted trillium, witch-hobble (hobblebush), blue-eyed grass, dog-hobble, simplex cinque-foil, dwarf cinquefoil, poor robin plantain, hooked buttercup, small ragwort, fleabane, rattlesnake weed, rue anemone, mountain fetter bush, Cherokee rose, corn salad, tulip tree, blueberry and huckleberry blooms, red-berried elder blooms.

JUNE — 16th, up Rainbow Falls Trail; sunny, hazy and sometimes cloudy with many birds singing; purple, dwarf and white rhododendron (beautiful between Rocky Spur and lodge), pink mountain laurel, galax, partridge-berry (white bloom), white sweet violet, wood sorrel, blackberries, enchanted nightshade, foamflower, saxifrage, tall meadow rue, sand myrtle, umbrella-leaf, witch-hobble (hobblebush), yellow clintonia, bluets, red-berried elder, wither rod bush. 17th, walked to Trillium Gap with Anita, seeing many of same flowers enjoyed yesterday on Rainbow Falls plus the purple fringed orchid; hard rain. 18th, down Alum Cave Bluff Trail, cloudy near top; cow parsnips, mountain laurel up high, many purple rhododendron above Alum Cave Bluff, few white rhododendron.

JULY — 12th, up Trillium Gap Trail, my 200th trip, sunny and cloudy; monkshood, red bee-balm, tall meadow rue, purple fringed orchid, turk's-cap lily and many white rhododendron at high elevations. 13th, at 5:00 a.m. saw crescent moon, Venus and another bright star, big dipper and then sunrise; down Boulevard trail with Anita, finding many monkshoods and bee balm, tall meadow rue, and few turk's-cap lillies up high. 14th, down Alum Cave Bluff Trail; purple rhododendron up high (past peak), saxifrage, St. John's-wort, grass of parnassus (early), wood sorrel, turtlehead, mountain mint, hydrangea, black snakeroot, many turk's-cap lillies beside highway after leaving trail head. Newspaper reporter was waiting in the parking lot to talk to me about the 200th trip.

AUGUST — 13th, up Trillium Gap Trail, partly cloudy but no rain; cohosh, snakeroot, bee balm, shaggy aster, monkshood, turtlehead, grass of parnassus, saxifrage, angelica, goldenrod, many green cone flowers; on top in afternoon walked back down Trillium Gap Trail to enjoy the grass of parnassus blooms, few pink turtleheads. 14th, down to flower garden on Boulevard; Stuart Bingham of Boulder, Colorado, my grand-nephew (age 21), and his friend Elizabeth Hayman hiked up Alum Cave to join me for the night (his fourth trip). 15th, down Bullhead with Stuart and Elizabeth (met several people going up the mountain who had seen me in a slide show at the park visitor center...they asked questions about my trips), saw saxifrage, mountain dandelion, St. John's-wort, grass of parnassus, goldenrod, lion's foot, false foxglove, gall of the earth, hairy bluebell, Canada violet, alum root, yellow fringed orchid, teaberry, white rhododendron, Joe Pye weed, ironweed, cohosh.

SEPTEMBER — 13th, up Rainbow Falls Trail; weather turbulent, rain more than one hour during ride, strong winds would open "windows" in clouds showing mountains in distance, valley usually engulfed in clouds, nearly blown off Rocky Spur, Le Conte summit not visible from there as usual, sand myrtle blooming on spur, grass of parnassus, red bee balm, yellow jewel weed; on top find lodge surrounded in dense clouds. 14th, awoke to see stars at 4:00 a.m., but clouds moved in to hide sunrise, stayed in writing notes on the trips and reading "Proverbs" in the Bible, in afternoon walked down Trillium Gap Trail to see grass of parnassus. 15th, down Bullhead, clouds heavy up high but no rain; grass of parnassus, red bee balm, yellow jewel weed, gentian, shabby and purple asters, snakeroot, green cone flowers, saxifrage, alum root, Canada violet, one precious yellow fringed orchid in full bloom on top of its stem.

OCTOBER — September 29th, up Rainbow Falls, late start because of delay in getting all members of riding party together; I developed headache, which improved upon reaching the lodge. Old friends Eula Fry and Millie Shields are there, having hiked up Alum Cave. They've come to help me celebrate my 86th birthday. Clouds cover the peaks and we sit in lodge reliving old times...at night could see stars through drifting clouds; 30th, weather partly clear, goodbye to Eula and Millie, back to bed to sleep 'til noon (headache much better), after lunch out to Myrtle Point with Anita to nap on rocks. Oct. 1, down Bullhead, cloudy on top, but sun shining at lower elevations; autumn colors beautiful, grass of parnassus, columbine, goldenrod, asters, gentians, Canada violet, Indian-pipe, saxifrage, hearts-a-bustin' seed are bright red, blueberries are ripe and we pick some and eat them as we walk along.

NOVEMBER — 1st, up Rainbow Falls Trail accompanied by Emilie Powell of Signal Mountain, Tennessee, who is riding a horse for the first time since childhood; broken clouds, windy, partly sunny, most autumn leaves gone except yellow birch, purple and shabby white asters, sun bright on Rocky Spur with clouds breaking to show expanses of mountains and lowlands, top of Le Conte is shrouded in clouds, arrive to find lodge in dense clouds. 2nd, cloud cover holds, walk with Emilie to hiking shelter, High Top, old barn and below the spring, say goodbyes to the staff until March, the lodge closes November 4 for the winter, Debbie and Rusty Nail will stay through the winter in their cabin below the dining hall. 3rd, down Bullhead with Emilie and the John Crabtrees, we leave in light drizzle which ends about midway; see witch hazel, purple and shabby white asters, Indian-pipe, gentian and witch-hobble (hobblebush); I thank God for another year of enjoying the beauty of Mount Le Conte.

About the Author

Emilie Ervin Powell of Signal Mountain, Tennessee, first climbed Mount Le Conte in 1956 while working in nearby Knoxville as a reporter for the *Knoxville Journal* and attending the University of Tennessee. In 1977, she ascended the mountain for the ninth time with Grace McNicol in preparation for writing the first edition of this book.

Ms. Powell was an editor with Provident Life and Accident Insurance Company in Chattanooga from 1960 to 1966. For the next 12 years, she was a freelance writer and editor of a magazine for Dixie Yarns, Inc. She joined the Tennessee Valley Authority in 1980 and worked as a business journalist until her retirement in 1994. Her duties involved editing TVA's *Industrial Digest* newsletter.

Ms. Powell has been active in the volunteer efforts of the Tennessee Trails Association to spearhead construction of the Cumberland Trail, a 185-mile scenic footpath which will eventually cross the state from Signal Mountain to Cumberland Gap, Kentucky. In addition, she is an active member of the Tennessee River Gorge Trust and the Chattanooga Audubon Society.